Books by Rick Riordan

www.rickriordan.co.uk

* *Also available as a graphic novel*

BROOKLYN HOUSE
MAGICIAN'S MANUAL

RICK RIORDAN

PUFFIN

A special thank-you to Stephanie True Peters
for her help with this book

PUFFIN BOOKS

UK | USA | Canada | Ireland | Australia India | New Zealand | South Africa

Puffin Books is part of the Penguin Random House group of companies
whose addresses can be found at global.penguinrandomhouse.com.

www.penguin.co.uk   www.puffin.co.uk   www.ladybird.co.uk

First published in the USA by Disney • Hyperion,
an imprint of Disney Book Group,
and in Great Britain by Puffin Books 2018

006

Text copyright © Rick Riordan, 2018
Illustrations by James Firnhaber
Hieroglyphs by Michelle Gengaro-Kokmen

The moral right of the author and illustrators has been asserted

Printed in Great Britain by Clays Ltd, ELCOGRAF S.P.A.

A CIP catalogue record for this book is available from the British Library

ISBN: 978-0-141-37771-1

All correspondence to:
Puffin Books, Penguin Random House Children's
80 Strand, London WC2R ORL

To all young magicians
May your wands never break
and your hieroglyphs always glow bright

CONTENTS

YOUR GUIDE TO

Egyptian Gods &
Creatures,
Glyphs & Spells
and More

A WORD OF WARNING

Agh!

TRANSLATION: Well, now you've done it. By finding this book, you've alerted nearby monsters and enemy magicians that you have magic powers. Soon they'll be coming after you. To escape, place your paw on the book's cover. A portal will open. Jump in. We'll be waiting on the other side to greet you (and hand you a Duat sickness bag if you need it).

Oh, and just so you know . . . things could get a little weird from here on in.

– Khufu, *resident baboon of Brooklyn House*

A little weird. Yeah, that's one way of putting it. – Sadie

3

NOTICE TO NEW ARRIVALS AT THE ROOFTOP PORTAL:

To avoid being devoured, please feed one (1) frozen turkey to Freak, our semi-domesticated griffin. Turkeys are located in the ice pyramid provided by Felix, trainee in slush, snow, ice and air-conditioning magic.

– Carter Kane

THE BOOK OF THIS BOOK
by Carter Kane

Greetings, initiate! Welcome to Brooklyn House. I'm Carter Kane. My sister, Sadie, and I are in charge here – and, yes, we really *are* siblings even though we look nothing alike. I take after our father, Julius, who has brown eyes and dark skin. That is, he *used* to have dark skin. It's more blue now . . . I'll explain why later. Sadie looks like our mother, Ruby – pale, blonde and blue-eyed. Mum's really pale now. Transparent, even. But then she's a ghost, so . . . yeah. – Sadie

Sadie and I don't sound alike, either. She has an English accent Um, no, Carter – you have an American accent. – Sadie because she grew up in London with our grandparents after Mom died. Meanwhile I travelled around with our dad, a famous Egyptologist. That might sound fun, but, trust me, living out of a suitcase got old quick.

That's all in the past now. Today Sadie and I live here in Brooklyn House, the headquarters of the Twenty-First Nome of the House of Life. A *nome* is a region or district. **Not a whimsical garden figurine with a pointy red hat. Common mistake. – Sadie** There are three hundred and sixty nomes in the *Per Ankh* – that's Egyptian for the House of Life, the ancient global organization of Egyptian magicians. Not pull-a-rabbit-out-of-a-hat magicians – people who can do *actual* magic. People like me and Sadie. And people like you. Surprise!

How do we know you can do magic? Because you found this book, and you made it here in one piece. These accomplishments signal that you have the blood of the pharaohs flowing through your veins. **You don't have the pharaohs' actual blood flowing through your veins. That would be disgusting, not to mention unsanitary. Just wanted to clarify that. – Sadie** That means you're descended from Ancient Egyptian royalty, and you have powers. Magic powers. More on that later, I promise. For now, I want to tell you how this book came about.

My girlfriend, Zia Rashid, and I were standing in line, ordering lunch at our favourite food-court restaurant. Suddenly Zia snatched a plastic knife and brandished it like a weapon. 'Carter, look! Someone is in trouble!'

I instantly tensed. 'What? Where? Who?'

She stabbed her utensil at a HELP WANTED sign by the cash register.

I relaxed. 'Yeah, um, that's not a cry for help, actually.' I explained that Meat on a Stick had job openings and handed her one of the application forms from the pile on the counter.

As she scanned the paper, her expression darkened. 'Good Ra, look at this.' She showed me the section marked PERSONAL INFORMATION. 'A devious trick to learn an applicant's *ren*, no doubt!'

A little background on Zia: she was raised by a two-thousand-year-old Egyptian magician in a secret headquarters hidden beneath Cairo. Some aspects of modern life are still mysterious to her.

I'm not wild about correcting my girlfriend – she has a rather fiery temper – but I feared she might attack the restaurant workers if I didn't. That would have been bad because 1) mall security frowns on the use of plasticware as deadly weapons, and 2) I was really hungry and wanted my food.

So I casually eased the knife from her fist and said, 'I don't think people who serve meat on a stick at a restaurant called Meat on a Stick are into secret names. They probably don't even know what a ren is, or the incredible power that comes with learning it.'

Unconvinced, Zia put the application on her food tray and brought it to our table, where she proceeded to read it aloud. '"Past Experience." Wouldn't you like to know,' she muttered between bites. '"Tell Us More About Yourself." No, I don't believe I will.'

Just then, my phone buzzed. I glanced at the text. 'Walt's asking us to come back to Brooklyn House. A bunch of new recruits just arrived.'

Let me pause for a moment to introduce you to Walt Stone. He's directly descended from King Tut, the world-renowned boy pharaoh with the treasure-filled tomb. Walt didn't inherit any treasure from his famous ancestor. (At least, I don't *think* he did.) But he did get something else: a death curse. Not too long ago he succumbed to that curse.

Okay, you might be asking yourself, *if Walt is dead, how did he text you? Is he a ghost?*

Answer: Walt is not a ghost – not that there's anything wrong with ghosts. My mother is one, and she's very nice. (There are nasty ghosts, too. The worst is Setne, an evil magician with delusions of immortality. Don't worry about him, though. He's imprisoned inside a snow globe on my desk. Feel free to give the globe a good shake some time. He hates that.) The

8

reason Walt is still around is because he merged with Anubis, the Egyptian god of death.

That last statement probably raises a second question: *What????*

Let me explain. To exist in our world, an Egyptian god needs a host. An artefact or an animal or even an element like water or earth will do, but most gods prefer to join with mortals. In exchange for sharing brain space, the human host, or *godling*, gains full access to the deity's power.

Sadie and I have been godlings. Zia, too – twice, actually. I'm not going to lie: having the power of a god is incredible. But merging with a deity can be very dangerous. **Disturbing, too, especially when the god tries to strike up a conversation in your head. Given a choice, I'll stick to my own inner monologue, thank you very much. – Sadie** Gods like to be in control. Let them into your mind, and they start pressuring you to do what *they* want. Resistance is almost impossible, and the risk of insanity and death by power overload is high. That's why we don't go the godling route any more – except for Walt, who is a special case because he is, technically, dead.

Okay, on with the story . . .

✦ ✦ ✦

Zia and I flew back to Brooklyn House courtesy of my griffin, Freak. As we dismounted – carefully, because his wings are deadly sharp – Walt joined us on the rooftop.

'How was Meat on a Stick?' he asked as we followed him down to the second-floor balcony.

'Delicious,' I said.

'Dangerous,' Zia corrected darkly. She waved the job application. 'I'm going to warn Sadie about this. Don't want her falling victim to such a trap.'

Once she was out of earshot, I filled Walt in about the mall incident. 'Zia knows so much about Ancient Egypt and magic that I forget she knows so little about modern life.'

'That's one advantage to my dual personality.' He tapped his head. 'Walt knows modern, and Anubis knows magic.'

'You're lucky.'

'*Dead* lucky,' he agreed.

Voices rose up from the Great Room, reminding me that we had new trainees. I peered down at them as they milled nervously around the thirty-foot-tall black marble statue of Thoth. I shook my head. 'How much do you think *they* know about the gods and goddesses or any of the magic stuff they're going to encounter here?'

'Not enough,' Walt said gravely. **Gravely. Very punny, Carter. – Sadie**

I leaned on the railing. 'So, they might misunderstand the most basic magical concepts. Just like Zia misunderstood the job application.'

'Probably.' Walt shrugged. 'But what can we do about it?'

I didn't answer because just then Sadie waltzed up to claim Walt. **Claim? You make me sound so possessive! I simply saw one of the recruits eyeballing my boyfriend and decided the sooner he knew Walt was mine, the better. – Sadie** I turned away from their public display of affection. My gaze fell on the items the statue of Thoth was holding – a papyrus scroll and a stylus – and then I knew the answer to Walt's question.

'A book!' I blurted.

Walt and Sadie broke apart. 'Don't look now,' Walt stage-whispered, 'but Carter is yelling out random nouns.'

'Better than some other things he could yell,' Sadie replied.

I rolled my eyes. 'I meant we should write a book about Egyptian magic.'

Sadie made a face. 'I don't *write*. I *talk*, and people listen.'

I ignored her. 'A book just for initiates. You know, so they have a clue about what they're getting into here. We'd explain the Duat, and the deities, and the path of the gods. Throw in some stories about our experiences. We could get the other Brooklyn House residents to contribute. Magicians from other nomes, too. And maybe . . .'

Sadie raised her eyebrows. 'The gods?'

I nodded. 'Yeah. The gods. So, what do you think? Should we write this book?'

Long story short, we wrote this book. I can't speak for everyone else, but I had fun putting it together. **The experience wasn't all bad, and my bits are quite worth reading. – Sadie** In fact, I'm thinking of writing a companion volume. I'll call it *Brooklyn House's Manual to Modern Life*. I know at least one magician who might find it useful. If you want to help, just stop by my room. Or visit me at Meat on a Stick. Apparently, someone filled out the job application in my name, and they want to hire me.

In the meantime, read on, initiate. And welcome to the world of Egyptian magic.

Hi. Sadie here, the younger and more fashion-forward

Kane sibling. Carter isn't usually irresponsible – I pride myself on leading in that category – so I was surprised he left the manuscript for this book unattended. And by 'unattended' I mean securely locked in his desk drawer. Honestly, anyone capable of casting a combination *sahad-w'peh* spell – that's *unlock-open* – could easily penetrate his worthless defences. As a follower of Isis, goddess of magic, I am more than capable, so, before you could say 'jelly baby', his papyrus was in my hands. Since words are my thing, I went ahead and added a few more. Then I bound them to his papyrus with a *hi-nehm* joining spell. I mean, I couldn't have Carter deleting my hard work now, could I?

AH, SADIE. YOU DIDN'T NOTICE THAT YOUR SAHAD–W'PEH SPELL NICKED MY SNOW-GLOBE PRISON, DID YOU, DOLL? YEAH, IT SPRANG A LEAK. WATER SEEPED OUT. WATER . . . AND ME, YOUR OLD PAL, SETNE.

SERIOUSLY, THOUGH, I OWE YOU AND CARTER BIG TIME FOR BRINGING ME INTO BROOKLYN HOUSE. I WOULDN'T BE HERE WITHOUT YOU. NOW I'M GOING TO ROAM AROUND AND LOOK FOR A CERTAIN BOOK YOU TOOK FROM ME. YOU KNOW THE ONE I MEAN. IT CONTAINS POWERFUL SPELLS, SECRET INFO ABOUT THE GODS – OH, AND MY PERSONAL FAVOURITE, INSTRUCTIONS FOR BECOMING IMMORTAL.

SPEAKING OF, I'VE GOT A WHOLE NEW APPROACH TO MY UNDYING QUEST FOR IMMORTALITY NOW. (UNDYING. HA! THAT'S A GOOD ONE. SOMEONE SHOULD BE WRITING THIS DOWN.) IT CAME TO ME AFTER YOU INTRODUCED ME TO A GUY WITH UNUSUAL POWERS. UNUSUAL FOR EGYPT, ANYWAY. LET ME TELL YOU, WHEN I TRANSFORM FROM GHOST TO GOD, IT'S REALLY GOING TO MAKE WAVES.

– SETNE

THERE'S NO PLACE LIKE NOME
by Carter Kane

B rooklyn House has everything fledgling magicians need to live and learn in comfort. It has some secrets, too. Let me explain.

Brooklyn House has been in our family for generations. Our dad and his younger brother, Amos, grew up here. Yet Sadie and I never knew the mansion existed until Uncle Amos transported us here in his magical boat – and we only came then because Dad had been imprisoned in a golden sarcophagus by Set, the god of evil, and we needed a safe place to stay. (Turns out it wasn't that safe, but we didn't discover that until later.)

The first morning Sadie and I spent at Brooklyn House, she literally blew the doors off the library so we could get a look inside. Since then, we've explored every part of this grand five-storey mansion, from the rooftop portal and the bedrooms to the training room, the infirmary and the Great Room. We've circled the wraparound terrace with its open-air dining facility and crocodile-length pool a dozen times. We've even peeked inside the supply cupboard and bathrooms. **Yeah, that doesn't make us sound creepy at all. – Sadie** We know every nook and cranny of Brooklyn House.

At least, we thought we did. Then we discovered a small trapdoor hidden beneath a rug on the ground floor. A small *locked* trapdoor that wouldn't open even when Sadie hit it with her most forceful *ha-di* spell. It takes some serious protective magic to hold up against that much destructive power.

Mystified, we contacted Uncle Amos to see if he knew anything about it. After all, he lived in our family mansion for years. In reply, he sent us an old cross-section drawing of Brooklyn House, made some time before it was elevated to its current position above the abandoned warehouse, along with this note:

> Kids,
> I'm flabbergasted by your find!
> *'Flabbergasted' would be a great word for a spell. – Sadie*
> Near as I can make out,
> Brooklyn House was originally

built over a *mastaba*, a type
of Ancient Egyptian tomb that
resembles a pyramid with the
point sliced off. Such tombs
had a shaft leading from a
rooftop opening to the actual
burial chamber located far
below the floor. The ground-
level floor had a secret room,
called a *serdab*, that held
a statue of the deceased's
ka, and another chamber with
afterlife offerings. Why a
mastaba was constructed beneath
Brooklyn House and whether
anyone was ever buried there
are mysteries to me. From
these sketches it seems the
trapdoor originally led into
the rooftop shaft opening.
Brooklyn House now hovers high
above the mastaba, but the two
may still be connected magically.
Which brings me back to the
trapdoor. The magic sealing

it shut is likely intended to
keep Brooklyn House residents
out . . . or to keep something
imprisoned within the mastaba.
If the latter, well, that
'something' - a ghost of a
long-dead Egyptian relative
would be my best guess -
probably won't be looking to
play patty-cake with you if it
gets out. So just STAY AWAY.
Best,
Amos

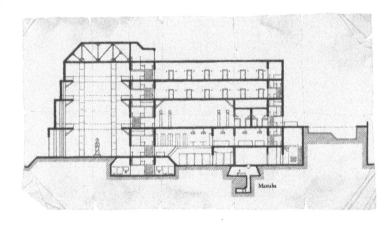

Mastaba

✦ ✦ ✦

Surprisingly, Sadie has stayed away. But I know she's still thinking about that trapdoor and who might lurk in the tomb beneath Brooklyn House. **You know me only too well! – Sadie** I am, too.

But don't worry. We've taken precautions to keep Brooklyn House residents safe. We added a *drowah* boundary spell around the trapdoor – that's the strange light in the corner – and beefed up the exterior hieroglyphs in case the whatever-or-whoever escapes and tries to circle back in. We've put Philip of Macedonia, our albino crocodile *shabti* — a figurine shaped out of wax and brought to life with magic — on high alert. Trust me: no ghost is going to get in through that trapdoor.

AN ANCIENT MASTABA WITH A POSSIBLY MALEVOLENT SPIRIT? NOW WE'RE TALKING! MORTAL MAGICIANS MIGHT NOT BE ABLE TO PENETRATE THAT MAGICAL TRAPDOOR, BUT A *GHOST* MAGICIAN? EASY-PEASY TAS-RIBBON SQUEEZY! – SETNE

SUPPLY CUPBOARD
by Doughboy

What are you staring at? You've never seen a lump of wax shaped like a man with no legs holding a clipboard before? You're eyeballing one hundred percent grade-A shabti here, my friend, so wipe that smile off your face and listen up.

Carter put me in charge of issuing equipment to new initiates. I take the job *very seriously*, because it gets me out of his magician's box. If you think it's fun being locked in a box all day, I've got a sarcophagus I'd like you to meet.

First on the list: clothing. Let's see what you brought with – Oh, you have *got* to be kidding me. A *goose-down* jacket? Give me that. Didn't anyone tell you clothes made from animals get in the way of magic? Don't even get me started on leather. And stop whining about your coat. Your wardrobe has a full supply of linen tops and bottoms. Last thing any of us wants is a house full of naked magicians.

Next item: a wand made of hippo ivory. Oh, you have your own, do you, big shot? Let me see that.

Hmm. Family heirloom? Nice etching on the sides. Images of Tawaret and Bes, if I'm not mistaken. Good protective symbols. I approve. It was broken at some point, but, judging by those ivory pegs, whoever did the repair, knew what he was doing. A fine piece. Don't dishonour it by using it like a boomerang. Oh, it happens. It happens.

Moving on: a wooden staff. I suppose you inherited one of those, too? No? What, did it explode or turn into a snake and slither off or snap in half? Yeah, they do that. They also get lost by numbskull magicians who expect their shabti to chase them down. So, keep an eye on the one I'm giving you. It's standard issue, unmarked, but once you start hurling spells with it hieroglyphs of your magical strengths should appear.

What else? Right, a magician's kit for supplies. You've got a choice of this wooden box – the lid's loose, lousy craftsmanship, I agree – or this leather satchel. What? Yeah, okay, smarty-pants, I know I said no leather. I can see I'll have to walk you through this, so pay attention. Leather clothes prevent magic. Leather satchels keep magic contained. Otherwise, the magic oozes out of the items. Trust me: you do *not* want to be walking around with a bag of oozing magic. Makes *isfet* of your clothes.

So, you want the box or – Don't grab! I've gotta fill your kit first! Sheesh. A ball of twine, a roll of papyrus, *menhed* – that's a scribe's palette with ink to you newbies – and your own shabti-making lump of wax. If you're not sure what to shape your lump into, I highly recommend a nice-looking half-lady. Wink, wink, ha, ha.

Last thing: an ivory headrest. You put your neck here, where it curves and – Don't give me that look. You'll get used to it. Honest to Ra, if you don't sleep with this every night, you'll regret it.

Okay, you're all set. Good luck with the whole path-of-the-gods thing. Next!

THE DO-*WHAT*?
by Carter Kane

M e again. I sent out a request for others to write this entry, but . . . well, me again. **Yeah, I binned that request. Sorry. (Not sorry.) – Sadie**

The Duat is a mysterious multi-layered realm of magic that flows just beneath our world. Magicians use the shallowest level for storing personal items. I put my *khopesh* and magician's box in the Duat, too – you know, stuff I want to keep safe or might need in a hurry. I also store the *djed* amulet my dad gave me in a locker there. The amulet is a little carving that looks like a spine. It symbolizes stability and strength. We use it as a beacon to summon new trainees, so you must have seen it when you found this book.

With proper training, you can use this Duat level to see another's hidden magical aspect. In the regular world, the thing might look perfectly normal. Lower your vision into the Duat, though, and that thing could appear very different. For instance, a moose once chased me through an airport – except it wasn't really a moose, it was a hideous monster. Sadie, who is better at peering into the Duat, can see Anubis, the god of death, superimposed on Walt. **Two hot guys in one package. Not bad, huh? – Sadie** This top layer is also good for rapid travel, via boat or *ba* – that's the personality part of your soul – or purple-hued magic portal.

The next Duat level down is the River of Night, the fabled waterway travelled by the sun god Ra on his nightly journey. The river passes some amazing sights. But steer clear until you've had a bit of magical training, because it also has some nasty surprises, like jagged rocks that can rip you apart, flame-filled water that can burn you to a crisp and, worst of all, a god named Shezmu who will squirt you in the face with nasty-smelling perfume.

Speaking of steering clear, avoid the deepest Duat levels. That's where the Sea of Chaos and the abyss are. I barely escaped the sea with my sanity intact. As for the abyss, well, if you're looking to vanish from existence, it's the place to be. Or not to be. Honestly, why would anyone want to go there? That is the question.

◆ ◆ ◆

A DJED AMULET? NIIIIICE. I COULD USE ONE OF THOSE.
USE IT UP *REAL* GOOD. AND MIGHT YOUR LOCKER ALSO
HIDE THE ANCIENT SCROLL I'VE BEEN SEARCHING FOR?
JUST GIVE ME THE COMBINATION, PAL, AND I'LL TAKE A
PEEK. – SETNE

TICKETS, PLEASE
by Bloodstained Blade

I found this papyrus on board our boat, the *Egyptian Queen*. Apparently, before the double-axe-headed captain was bound in service to our family, he was a tour guide. Who knew? – Carter

Good evening, and welcome to the *Spirit of the Duat*, the flagship of the River of Night cruise line. I am your demonic guide, Bloodstained Blade, and I will do my best to kill you during this trip – er, *protect* you during this trip, I mean. I will do my best to kill you at the *end* of the tour.

Please note that those signed up for the guided ba experience of the Duat should now remove the protective ivory headrests from their beds and fall asleep. Failure to comply will result in missing the tour. No refunds.

Our live-action adventure sets off from the First House dock precisely at sunset. We then travel through the rather boring Second and Third Houses to the Fourth House, where the Sunny Acres

Assisted-Living Community is located. You'll have exactly one visiting hour there. Say hello to Nurse Hippo, but just say no to any of her needles. If you do not return to the boat within sixty minutes, plan to spend the next twenty-three hours rubbing elbows with long-forgotten and always-forgetful deities.

From Sunny Acres we head into the always-entertaining Land of the Dead. (Well, entertaining for me, anyway, as this is where I often lose a passenger or two.) Take a dip in the Lake of Fire, have a snack with Osiris, the god of the Underworld, and then see him at work in the Hall of Judgement, located on his island oasis. Again, visits at each place will be of limited duration. If you wish to stay longer than the time allotted, you must schedule a game of senet with Khonsu, the moon god. Have your ren ready.

Once you're back on board – or not – we'll pick up our tour with the Fifth House. Then the Sixth. Then Seventh, Eighth and . . . well, you get the point. Or perhaps the blade, if I'm sneaky enough. Our tour will conclude at the Twelfth House, where you will witness a glorious sunrise. Your last, if I have my way.

Well, I see the crew lights are preparing for departure, so at this time we ask you to stow your magician's boxes in a secure magical location and to listen carefully to the following safety guidelines:

1. Keep hands, feet, heads and other dangling appendages inside the vessel at all times. Sunglasses, hats and fake beards should be removed prior to departure. Management is not responsible for lost items, limbs or lives.

2. The Duat is home to a wide variety of indigenous mythical creatures. Some are harmless. Others are quite harmful. We invite you to admire or fear these creatures from a safe distance. Flash photography and screaming are discouraged, as these activities disturb the demons.

3. While we anticipate a smooth journey, chances are we'll inadvertently spring at least one hidden trap. Or perhaps the trap will be sprung advertently. In the event of a deadly emergency, menheds with a chart of protective hieroglyphs will materialize before you. Paint the appropriate glyph on

your own forehead first, then on those of
any children travelling with you.

Thank you for your attention to these matters. Now,
without further ado, I invite you to sit back, relax and
prepare to enjoy your last night alive. I mean, prepare
to enjoy the River of Night. And please remember to
tip your tour guide on your way out so that you'll be
within easy striking distance.

BSB! I *hate* that demon! I bet he'd lend a blade to our
worst enemy in a heartbeat. I'm glad he's still deep in the
Duat. – Sadie

BSB! I *LOVE* THAT DEMON! I BET HE'D LEND ME A BLADE
AGAINST THE KANES IN AN *IB*-BEAT. WHICH IS WHY I'M
GOING TO PAY HIM A LITTLE VISIT DEEP IN THE DUAT.

– SETNE

IN THE ZONE
by Carter Kane

I'll never forget Sadie's and my first training lesson. It took place at the First Nome in Cairo – the main headquarters and original training grounds for magicians of the House of Life. That lesson included having our tongues painted with a foul-tasting hieroglyph that was supposed to help us enunciate spells clearly. I don't know about Sadie, but I was too busy gagging to say anything other than *blecch*. **Carter still sounds like he's gagging when he tries to do spells, poor lamb. – Sadie**

Here at Brooklyn House, training takes a different path – the path of the gods, a unique connection forged between a magician and a god in which the magician channels the god's magic to amplify his own abilities. We'll help you learn to make that link, starting with some tips I got from an unusual source.

I was lying on the sofa in the Great Room of Brooklyn House one night, pondering how to explain the path of the gods for this book, when a hairy weight dropped on my chest.

'Oof! Khufu!'

'*Agh!*' Our baboon grunted an apology – at least I *think* it was an apology; he could have been reciting Hamlet's soliloquy for all I know – then grabbed my hand and pulled me upstairs to our indoor basketball court. Scattered around the hardwood floor were four purple Los Angeles Lakers jerseys, like the one Khufu was wearing, and four green Boston Celtics shirts. A basketball sat in the centre circle.

'*Agh.*' Khufu shoved a sheet of papyrus into my hands, gestured towards the jerseys and stared at me expectantly. I shrugged, not understanding. He made an exasperated face and stabbed a finger at the papyrus.

The paper was covered in hieroglyphs. I knew it was a spell of some kind, but it took me a moment to decipher it. 'Hang on. Khufu . . . will this spell bring those jerseys to life?'

Khufu flashed me a *yeah, duh* look.

I had first-hand experience with animated clothing, having ridden in a boat piloted by Uncle Amos's enchanted trench coat. I could guess why Khufu wanted me to rouse the jerseys. See, I love basketball. I have a decent shot as long as I'm alone on the court. Put a defender on me, though, and I choke.

Same with dribbling, passing, rebounding – pretty much all facets of the game, sadly. Stinking up the court was bad enough, but even worse were the sideways glances I got from Khufu and his basketball-playing baboon buddies.

But now I had the chance to practise my moves without being sucker-punched by judgemental looks. 'Okay, here goes nothing.'

Nothing is pretty much what happened when I recited the spell. The shirts just swished across the floor like dust rags. I concentrated harder and read the spell again. Result! The jerseys rose up and hung in the air at player chest height. A black-and-white referee shirt appeared with a whistle floating where the official's mouth would have been.

'*Agh.*' Khufu tossed me a Boston jersey – number 33, last worn by Celtics great Larry Bird. Not my favourite team, but I respected Bird. I tugged it on, then followed Khufu to the centre circle for the opening tip-off. The ref shirt wafted over and picked up the ball with its invisible hand.

'Gotta love Egyptian magic,' I muttered.

The ref gave a blast on the whistle and tossed the ball straight up. Khufu got the upper hand – er, *paw* – and flipped the ball towards his teammate.

What followed was the weirdest game of basketball I've ever played. Weird and mortifying because, as always, I was awful. I dribbled off my foot. I clanged my jump shots and ricocheted my lay-ups. I made lousy across-the-key passes that were picked off and reversed downcourt for thunderous Laker dunks.

My highlight – or lowlight – moment came near half-time. As the Laker shirts zipped the ball around the key, I lunged to intercept a hard pass, tripped and caught the ball with the side of my head. I was out before my face kissed the floor.

'Not sure I want this guy wearing my jersey.'

'Well, they can't play shirts and skins, because no one has skin.'

At the sound of voices, I groaned and opened my eyes.

Two ba hovered over me. One had a Bird head – a *Larry* Bird head, that is. The other one's head was Magic, as in Magic Johnson, superstar Laker and one of my all-time favourite players. In fact, I'd used his jersey number, 32, and those of two other Laker greats, Wilt Chamberlain, 13, and Kareem Abdul-Jabbar, 33, as my Duat locker combination.

I started to sit up, but the Bird ba held up a

cautioning wing. 'I wouldn't do that. Not unless you want to pass out again.'

I stayed down. 'What are you guys doing here?'

'Came to give you some pointers, man,' Magic said.

'Oh, okay.' I mean, what else was I going to say – *Um, no thanks, I've got plenty of game without your help?*

Magic settled onto the floor next to me. 'First off, you've got to find a position that works with your natural abilities. You're trying to be a centre. No offence, but you don't have the height. Don't try point guard, either, because your ball-handling skills leave something to be desired right now. Try shooting guard, or maybe small or power forward.'

'Work on your fundamentals,' Bird put in. 'As a great man once said, "A winner is someone who recognizes his God-given talents, works his tail off to develop them into skills, and uses these skills to accomplish his goals."' He preened. 'It's a famous quote. I'm sure you've heard it.'

'No,' I admitted. 'Who said it?'

Bird frowned. 'I did.'

Magic nearly busted a gizzard laughing. 'Love it! But Bird's right. Practise your fundamentals until you can do them in your sleep. And make sure you have at least one go-to shot.'

'Team chemistry is important, too,' Bird added. 'If you don't mesh with your teammates, you've lost before you've even hit the court.'

'Position, fundamentals, go-to shot, team chemistry. Got it,' I replied.

'One more tip.' Magic put a wing on my shoulder. 'Relax. Go with the flow. *Feel* the game.'

Bird nodded. 'It's the only way you'll get in the zone.'

'In the zone.' I nodded. 'Yeah, I'd like to get there. Anything else?'

'*Agh*,' Bird said.

'Um, sorry, I didn't quite get that,' I replied.

Bird nudged Magic. 'The kid's waking up for real. Time for us to fly.' He flapped his wings and took off.

'You trying to beat me to the basket? No chance!' Magic flew after him.

'Wait! Come back!'

I sat up too fast. My head swam, and down I went.

✦ ✦ ✦

'*Agh!*'

I awoke to Khufu pressing a cold cloth to my forehead. He bared his teeth in a smile, patted my shoulder and turned away, giving me an uncomfortably close look at his multicoloured rump. I sat up gingerly, but the cloth must have been soaked in some magical concussion cure, because I felt great.

Better than great, actually, because I'd solved the problem of explaining the path of the gods. So here it goes.

The path of the gods starts with matching your personality, talents and interests with a deity – just like finding a position that suits your abilities on the court. You practise channelling your deity's magic to get better at controlling the flow of power – just as you practise the fundamentals in basketball. You find a go-to spell or magic speciality just like you find a go-to shot. Basketball teams need good chemistry; a god–magician team needs a sympathetic bond – a shared feeling, experience or common goal – for the magical connection to be truly successful.

And in both the path of the gods and basketball you've *got* to relax and go with the flow. If you resist, you'll never get into the magic zone.

Oh, and for those of you wondering how the

second half of the game went? Celtics over Lakers by one, thanks to a buzzer beater by yours truly.

A sports analogy? Really? Well, I guess it works. Oh, and by the way – Khufu was recording the game. Your lowlight moment was the highlight of my night! – Sadie

THE PATH OF THE GODS. YEAH, I THOUGHT ABOUT GOING DOWN THAT ROUTE WHEN I WAS ALIVE. TURNS OUT I DON'T LIKE SHARING POWER.

BUT YOU LIKE SHARING, CARTER, AND THAT'S GOOD NEWS FOR ME. GOT MY HANDS ON YOUR DJED AMULET THANKS TO THOSE NUMBERS YOU SHARED. A LITTLE DISAPPOINTED THE BOOK OF THOTH WASN'T IN YOUR LOCKER, THOUGH. BUT I'LL FIND IT. SOONER OR LATER . . . I'LL FIND IT. – SETNE

THE
FIRST
FAMILY
OF
GODS
AND
GODDESSES

AN APOLOGY TO THE GODS
by Carter Kane

Regrettably, we could not include all the Egyptian deities in this book. They number in the hundreds, maybe thousands, so the book would be a foot thick **Or, as we Brits would say, about thirty centimetres – Sadie** and weigh a ton **Or, as we Brits would say, that's an exaggeration – Sadie.** So, we stuck with those deities we've met, battled or shared brain space with. Our apologies to those we left out.

And, FYI, the god quizzes were my idea. A lousy idea, according to Sadie – 'Stupid Isfet, Carter, we get enough tests at BAG!' – but the Brooklyn Academy for the Gifted won't teach you this stuff, so I kept them in. Sadie gave you the answers, anyway. Well, sort of. I've tried to correct her answers, but if you have questions come and see Zia or me.

THE QUIZ OF RA

Interesting story: around about 1352 BCE a pharaoh named Akhenaten tried to do away with the worship of all the gods except the sun god, whom he called Aten. That one-god religion only lasted as long as Akhenaten was alive, though. His successor, King Tut, switched back to the old ways.

Circle the correct answer:

1. Ra is a) the god of the sun; b) the first king of the gods; c) the god of creation; d) all of the above.

2. Which of these names is *not* associated with Ra? a) Amun-Ra; b) Khepri; c) Elvis; d) Khnum.

3. Which animals are sacred to Ra? a) baboon and ibis; b) vulture and crocodile; c) scarab and ram; d) platypus and rat.

4. Ra's preferred mode of travel is a) a limousine littered with fast-food trash; b) a boat manned by glowing spheres of light; c) a sun chariot; d) a farting camel.

5. Ra's mortal form is a) an impossibly old bald man with golden eyes; b) a rainbow-wigged clown; c) an enormous baboon; d) a loincloth-wearing blue-skinned giant.

6. Ra's avatar is a) a much larger but still impossibly old bald man with golden eyes; b) an incandescent light too bright to look at directly; c) a massive dung beetle; d) all of the above.

7. Ra's magical speciality is a) fire; b) flailing his flail; c) charm-making; d) gnawing on his crook.

8. Ra nearly died once. How, where, and by whose hand? a) Colonel Mustard in the conservatory with the *netjeri*; b) Isis on the sun boat with snake venom; c) Apophis in the Duat with his fangs; d) It's a trick question – Ra 'dies' nearly every day at dawn.

Answers:

1. **d:** Ra is one busy deity! We'd also accept an alte-native answer of 'god of *Ma'at*, order in the universe'.

2. **c:** Though worshipped the world over, Elvis is not, technically, a god. Khepri is Ra's aspect in the morning. Khnum is his aspect at sunset. Amun-Ra is just a fancy way of saying Ra.

3. **c:** I can see ram – head-butting power and all that. But scarab, a beetle that rolls its own poop into a ball? Really?

4. **b:** The limo belongs to Bes, who you'll learn about later. The sun chariot belongs to a different sun god with connections on Long Island. As for the farting camel . . . you do not want to know.

5. **a:** We're talking *old*, though he was looking a bit healthier when we last saw him. The baboon is called Babi, and the blue giant, who we sincerely hope still has his loincloth, is Hapi, a minor god of the Nile.

6. **b:** I know, I wanted the answer to be c, too.

7. **a:** He's pretty good at gnawing and flailing, to be honest. Actually, I don't know if he has *sau* abilities.

8. **b:** A netjeri is a black blade made from meteoric iron. We'd also accept *d*, though we hope this 'death' is something you never witness, because it is freaky beyond compare.

ONE IS THE
LONELIEST NUMBER
by Zia Rashid

All right, Zia, just speak into this –
Heqat! Whack!

Ooohhh. *Thud.*

Whoops. Carter?

Well, he's unconscious. Let me just . . .

[*Sound of a body being dragged across a floor. Murmurs. Footsteps approaching.*]

Thanks, Jaz, I'll come check on him in a minute! Shoot, is this thing still recording?

Um, hi. Zia here. Let me explain what just happened. Carter shoved something in my face. I thought he was attacking, and instinct took over. I summoned my staff and swung and . . . Well, Jaz, our expert *rekhet*, or healer, is tending his head wound. Turns out the thing he shoved at me was this microphone.

So, anyway . . . Carter suggested I record my story rather than write it down. Apparently, my spoken words are easier to transcribe than my written hieroglyphs. I offered to use the more pedestrian hieratic or even – *shudder* – the lowly demotic script.

He pointed out that recording would save papyrus. Point taken.

He also suggested that it would be helpful if I 'spilled my guts'. That is not going to happen. Gut-spilling is disgusting. I should know. I was recently involved in one, courtesy of Apophis, the exploding serpent of Chaos. I do *not* recommend it.

Besides, it will be more helpful if I tell you about the birth of existence.

At the beginning there was a great magical swirl of monumental nothingness: the Sea of Chaos, sometimes known as Isfet. From Isfet came Ma'at, the force of order and creation borne of madness and destruction. Isfet and Ma'at were in perfect balance and perfect opposition to one another. Like two sides of the same coin, one could not exist without the other.

In time two gods emerged. Apophis squirmed out of the Sea of Chaos and slithered to the darkest depths of the abyss, where he writhed in constant fury and hate. And from Ma'at rose Ra, the god of the sun.

Ra's warmth and light spread outward through Ma'at, probing the empty space that surrounded him.

But his warmth and light touched nothing and no one. Ra was alone.

Tradition says that's when he created Shu and Tefnut – brother and sister, husband and wife, wind and rain. But I know better, because Ra and I were once connected. Being his host gave me the opportunity to see creation through his memories. I felt him pull back his warmth and light from the void and search inward for companionship instead. So I can attest that before Shu and Tefnut came Khepri and Khnum – sunrise and sunset – borne out of his loneliness.

The three were inseparable yet separate. Khepri rejuvenated Ra each dawn, then sent him on his way across the daytime sky. Khnum met him each evening at the end of his trip, then bade him farewell as Ra began his nightly journey through the Duat.

Ra's loneliness was lessened by their presence, but not erased completely. He burned to share Ma'at with others. Others who were different from him, and who could bring complexity to his existence, not just reflect back the sameness of his own world.

That's when he created Shu and Tefnut. They gave birth to Geb and Nut, and in time others followed: gods and goddesses, demons and beasts.

Humans. Plants. Beetles who roll their own poop into balls. And the rest, as they say, is mythology.

Why did I choose this story out of all those about Ra? Because it speaks to the path of the gods. Ra chose me as his host in part because I am a powerful fire elementalist. But our bond went deeper than that. When I was a child, my family was torn from me. I was alone, as Ra once was. My loneliness, Ra's loneliness . . . our shared feeling connected us, and together we were strong.

Okay, I'm done now. Is this the right button to turn this thing –

I've been meaning to ask Zia about Ra's connection to the part of the soul called the *sheut*, shadow. (The other four parts are ba, personality; ka, life force; ren, secret name; and ib, heart.) Are sheuts made by Ra's sunlight more, er, soulful than those made by, say, light from a torch – a *flashlight*, as you Americans call it? And I have a part two to ask: does Ra have a sheut, and, if so, how does the god of the sun cast his own shadow? – Sadie

THE QUIZ OF TEFNUT

Tefnut's husband, Shu, the god of the air, appears in our world as a whirlwind of trash and debris. So what would Tefnut manifest herself as – a puddle or a drain spout or an umbrella, maybe?

Fill in the blanks:

1. Tefnut is the goddess of <u>Who knows? I've never even heard of her!</u>

    The correct answer is *rain and moisture*.

2. Tefnut is the sister of <u>Is it Shu? No, wait, it can't be, because Shu is Teflon's husband.</u>

    The correct answer is *Shu*, who is both her brother and her husband. And her name is Tef*nut*, not Tef*lon*.

Okay, can you blame me for not wanting this to be the answer? I mean, Carter is *my* brother, so. . . ew. – Sadie

3. Tefnut is the mother of <u>**a farting camel.**</u>

    The correct answer is *Geb and Nut,* neither of whom is a camel, though they might fart for all we know.

4. Tefnut has the appearance of <u>**I'm going to go ahead and refer you to my answer to question number 1 here.**</u>

    The correct answer is *a lion-headed goddess,* which we agree is an odd look for the goddess of rain and moisture.

5. Her magical speciality is <u>**being the deity no one knows about. Seriously, why is she even included in this book?**</u>

    The correct answer is *water elementalism.* At least we assume it is. We've never actually seen her in action. We've included her in this book because she is a member of the first family of deities.

THE QUIZ OF SHU

True or False?

1. Shu is the god of wind and air.

    True   False

2. Shu couldn't wait to become a grandfather.

    True   False

3. Shu wears a falcon feather.

    True   False

Answers:

1. **True.** He also whips up a mean dust devil.

2. **False.** On Ra's orders, Shu used his wind power to blow apart his kids, Geb and Nut, so they couldn't conceive their own children. The tactic failed. Result: Isis, Osiris, Set and Nephthys. Plus someone called Horus the Elder, who must have taken a back seat to Horus the Warrior, because we never hear about him.

3. **False.** Shu wears an ostrich feather, which probably blew in from another region of Africa.

BLOW ME AWAY
by Leonid, from St Petersburg, Russia

Shu is born when Ra sneezed, I hear. I think for this reason I am glad that I do not ever host Shu. He would maybe turn my brain to sticky. I say *nyet* to that.

Tefnut would be no fun, too. She is from spit of Ra.

I think sometimes it is a strange thing, this magic of Egypt.

I have no clue where Leonid got this information. But I'm sure it was very good, very reliable, probably the best source ever, not fake mythology like you'd get from other sources. – Sadie

THE QUIZ OF NUT AND GEB

My student Alyssa and I insisted that these two share a quiz. After being apart for millennia, it only seemed fair.

— Sadie

Match the terms to the deities:

1. 'Twinkle, Twinkle, Little Star'

      Geb   Nut

2. Sandbox

      Geb   Nut

3. Downward dog

      Geb   Nut

4. Eluded magicians

      Geb   Nut

5. Earthquakes

    Geb   Nut

6. Won five extra days

    Geb   Nut

7. Glow-in-the-dark stick-on galaxies

    Geb   Nut

8. Dirt cake

    Geb   Nut

9. Cursed by Ra

    Geb   Nut

Answers:

1. **Nut**: She's the goddess of the starry sky.

2. **Geb:** God of the earth, including sand.

3. **Nut:** She's usually portrayed in this type of position, arched over those below her.

4. **Nut:** The sky proved too immense for magicians to capture.

5. **Geb:** Earth god = earthquakes

6. **Nut:** According to myth, Ra didn't want her to have kids. He cursed her so she couldn't give birth on any of the days of the year. Nut gambled with Khonsu, the moon god and god of time, for extra days. She won.

7. **Nut:** Followers of her path love these things!

8. **Geb:** Followers of his path love this dessert – crushed-up Oreos mixed with chocolate pudding and studded with gummy worms, all put in a plastic bucket. Delish!

9. **Geb and Nut:** Yet another failed attempt by Ra to keep them from having kids. See *Shu* entry.

THE QUIZ OF OSIRIS

The gods tend to repeat their history. Way back when – like, way, *way* back – Set, the god of evil, trapped his brother Osiris in a coffin. Why? Because he's the god of evil. A few years ago he sprang the same trap again, only this time he captured Osiris *and* his human host in the prison. If you've been paying attention, you'll know who that host was. If not . . . take the quiz and you'll find out.

Circle the correct answer:

1. Osiris is a) hosted by Julius Kane; b) blue, as in the colour, though possibly mood as well; c) the god of the Underworld; d) all of the above.

2. Osiris is the father of a) Shezmu;
    b) Disturber; c) Ammit; d) Horus.

3. The symbol of Osiris is the a) *was*;
    b) *sahlab*; c) *djed*; d) *bennu*.

4. His primary residence is a) Sunny Acres
    Assisted-Living Community; b) the Land
    of Demons; c) a golden sarcophagus;
    d) the Seventh House of the River of
    Night in the Land of the Dead.

5. His primary workplace is a) Sunny Acres
    Assisted-Living Community; b) the Hall of
    Judgement; c) a papyrus-making factory;
    d) the British Museum.

6. His favourite mortal child is a) Sadie;
    b) Sadie; c) Sadie; d) all of the above.

Answers:

1. **d:** Yeah, that's our dad, all right. Long ago, Osiris was banished deep in the Duat with the other gods. Dad released him, and Osiris took him as his host. Due to circumstances beyond their control, that became a permanent gig. So, technically, our dad is both Osiris and Julius Kane.

2. **d:** Shezmu is a demon god of the River of Night. Disturber is a minor Underworld god and Dad's right-hand man. Ammit is a monster that dines on the hearts of the unworthy dead and yet somehow is still adorable.

3. **c:** The was is a symbol of power. Sahlab is a hot beverage consumed in Egypt. The djed is the symbol of strength, stability and the rebirth of Osiris. A bennu is a phoenix.

4. **d:** Sunny Acres is a retirement community run by our dear friend and hippo goddess Tawaret. The Land of Demons is . . . well, that should be obvious. We would also have accepted c, because Osiris did once reside in a golden sarcophagus. But it was only temporary, and we try not to talk about it.

5. **b:** Is there such a thing as a papyrus-making factory?

6. **d:** Grrr, Sadie! This question wasn't in the original

quiz! 😊 – Sadie

GET WITH THE PROGRAMME
by Sadie Kane

As the god of the Underworld, Dad – or Osiris, if you insist on formalities – decides whether the deceased deserve to spend eternity in Aaru (paradise) or have their hearts devoured (not paradise). It's an important job, but I bet it gets a little tedious. So, brilliant girl that I am, I thought: *Why not give the procedure a little bounce by modelling it on a reality courtroom television programme?* You know the ones: Judge Somebody-or-other strides in, all puffed-up, black robes sweeping the floor, and listens to one dodgy individual accuse another dodgy individual of perpetrating a crime against him. After some shouting, aggressive finger-pointing and Sobek – er, crocodile tears, the judge mocks both parties and then offers up a binding and legal decision on who was in the wrong. Great stuff. You can see what I mean the next time you're off sick from school.

In the meantime, check out this sample episode of *In the Hall* (working title) I sent to Dad.

In the Hall

[Dramatic theme music and title sequence: a montage of close-ups of Dad, Ammit, some unsavoury-looking people and the Feather of Truth]

Scene: The Hall of Judgement. An empty throne sits on a golden dais. To the right is a set of scales. To the left lolls Ammit, the adorable crocodile-lion-hippopotamus mash-up who devours the hearts of unworthy souls. A handful of spectral spectators sit in the courtroom. Cameo by Mum if she wants!

VOICEOVER: Welcome to the Hall of Judgement. The case you are about to witness is real. The plaintiff and the defendant are dead, but their grievances live on. The judgement for or against is final.
[Dramatic theme music]

Scene: Enter Disturber, a decrepit-looking blue-skinned minor god of the Underworld with a truly hideous Egyptian-style toupee.

DISTURBER: All rise for the honourable Judge Osiris!

Scene: Dad walks in looking regal in his full Osiris kit – linen kilt, gold and coral neckbands, sandals, crook and flail in hand – and takes a seat on the throne.

OSIRIS: Right. What's first on the docket?

DISTURBER: Wrongful death suit.
[Dramatic theme music]

Scene: Two ghosts enter. The plaintiff wears an outdated sailor's uniform. The defendant is dressed in traditional magician's garb with an amulet for maw, *water, around his neck.*

DISTURBER: The English sailor claims the Egyptian magician caused his death in the Bay of Biscay.

OSIRIS: Bay of Biscay . . . Why does that sound familiar?

DISTURBER *[clears throat uncomfortably]*: Ah, that would be because of Cleopatra's Needle.
[Historic theme music]

VOICEOVER: Cleopatra's Needle: a gift from the Egyptian government to the people of Great Britain. On 8 September 1877 the immense red granite obelisk was loaded inside a specially constructed iron cylinder. A British ship, the *Olga*, towed it from the port of Alexandria across the Mediterranean Sea to the Bay of Biscay where, on 14 October, a storm halted its journey. Mammoth waves battered the cylinder, threatening to sink it. Six members of the *Olga*'s crew – including the plaintiff – perished trying to save the obelisk. The cylinder was finally cut from its tether and presumed lost at sea. Amazingly, it was discovered four days later floating off the coast of Spain, its precious cargo still inside. After months of delay, the cylinder was towed to London. The obelisk was finally erected on the banks of the Thames on 12 September 1878.

[Dramatic theme music]

OSIRIS: Hello, sailor. State your case.

SAILOR: Well, I was doin' me job, wasn't I? Trying to save that iron cigar wiv the stone monument, when out of nowhere comes this bloke. *[Jabs finger towards the Egyptian magician]* I turns to me mates and says, 'Who's this, then?' No answer, because before you can say Bob's your uncle, the daft Egyptian waves his stick, and the cylinder heaves us into the drink!

Osiris: And what happened to you next?

Sailor: Thrashed about a bit then drowned, didn't I?

Osiris: Ah, yes, of course. Magician, what have you to say?

Magician: I am the descendant of the pharaoh Ramesses II. That obelisk is carved with inscriptions honouring his victories. I –

Sailor: Blimey! Get him: descendant of the pharaoh. Like he's all that.
[Smattering of laughter from the courtroom]

Magician *[glowering at the sailor]*: The obelisk was my gateway to the god Horus, whom the Great Ramesses once hosted. I lived in its shadow for years, drawing on its power.

Osiris: Its shadow? Forgive me, but wasn't the obelisk buried in the sand for centuries before the English dug it out? *[More laughter]*

MAGICIAN *[now glowering at Osiris]*: It was *mine*! Egypt had no right to give it away.

OSIRIS *[pyramiding fingers]*: I see. Judging by your amulet, I'm guessing your magical speciality is water elementalist.

MAGICIAN: The best that ever lived.

SAILOR: The best *what-ever* died, more like. *[Laughter]*

OSIRIS: Quiet in the court!

SAILOR: Sorry, guv.

OSIRIS: So, magician, I presume you went to the bay to retrieve the obelisk.

MAGICIAN: Yes! And I would have succeeded had I done my magic from land.

OSIRIS: Ah, but you were forced to go on the open sea. Magic moves with much greater force over flowing water. Away from solid ground, amid the churning waves – you couldn't handle that much power. You lost control of the cylinder. And men died, including the plaintiff here.

MAGICIAN: Well, I . . . er, I don't know anything about that.

OSIRIS: Disturber, the Feather of Truth, please.

MAGICIAN: Okay, fine! Yes, I caused the storm, I lost control, and men died, including the plaintiff.

SAILOR: Oi! You all heard him! It's a fair cop! He is not worthy! Eat his heart out, Poochiekins!

OSIRIS: Silence! I alone give Poochiekins – er, *Ammit* – the order to devour a heart!
[Dramatic theme music]

VOICEOVER: Osiris's decision . . . when we return.
[Advert break]

I ask you, is that good drama or what? With an excellent cliffhanger, I might add.

And in case you were curious: the Needle *is* connected to Ramesses II. Six men died during its transport to London. The stuff about descendants of the pharaoh getting a power boost when they're near the Needle is also true. I know, because I'm descended from Ramesses II on my mother's side, and I've felt that energy. Carter gets a double dose: as Ramesses's descendant, and because, like Ramesses, he once hosted Horus. As for a magician causing the storm and the sailors' deaths, there's no evidence of that. But I wouldn't be surprised to learn that magic had something to do with the tragedy.

SADIE, YOU DOLL, THANKS FOR THE TIP! JUST PAID DEAR OL' DAD'S MONUMENT A LITTLE VISIT AND, I GOTTA SAY, I FEEL RECHARGED! – SETNE

THE QUIZ OF SET

Many Egyptian gods appear with the heads of recognizable animals – an ibis, a falcon, a crocodile, a jackal. Set has an animal head too, but, unlike the others, no one has ever been able to identify the animal it comes from. Somehow this just makes him seem all the more evil to me.

Fill in the blanks:

1. Set is _a lowdown, nasty, manipulative, vicious, scheming snake in the grass!_

> While this is an accurate summation of Set's character, the answer we were looking for is *the god of evil*. Points

deducted, though, for calling him a snake. That description is reserved for Apophis, the serpent of Chaos.

2. Set's favourite colour is <u>red, red and more red, from the darkest shade to . . . well, not pink but maybe fuchsia if he's in the mood to make a bold fashion statement.</u>

   This is the correct answer. As for fashion, however, it should be noted that his three-piece suit was black the last time we saw him.

3. Set's three most recent hosts were <u>Uncle Amos, the red pyramid of Arizona (destroyed in Washington DC) and, um, the malachite jar in Vladimir Menshikov's office?</u>

   This is a trick question aimed at revealing other hosts Set may have sneaked into during his last stay in the mortal world. Uncle Amos and the red pyramid were two; 'malachite jar' is a surprisingly good response.

4. Set's avatar is <u>half sandstorm, half fire, all lowdown, nasty, manipulative, vicious, scheming giant red warrior.</u>

This is the correct, though somewhat hyperbolic, answer.

5. Set has a special monster called **Leroy.**

   Leroy is the name I gave the monster. Its actual name is the Set animal. A weird mash-up of creatures, it has an anteater-shaped head with razor-sharp teeth and conical ears that swivel in all directions, a body as muscular as a greyhound's but as big as a horse, and a reptilian tail with triangular points at the end. Am I surprised that such a grotesque creature is named after the god of evil? I am not.

6. Though their names sound alike, Set should not be confused with **Leroy.**

   Excuse me, but in what universe does *Set* sound like *Leroy*? The correct answer is *Setne.* It's easy to confuse them since both are nasty and manipulative. But Set is a god; Setne is a magician. Or was. Now he's a ghost stuck inside a plastic snow globe.

Bonus question: Set has suggested two
alternatives, Rockin' Red Reaper and Glorious
Day, to his true secret name, Evil Day. Can you
suggest others? I think 'Murray' would put a crimp
in his style. I'm going to call him that from now on.

THE TO-UNDO LIST

FROM THE DESK OF AMOS KANE, CHIEF LECTOR,

FIRST NOME, SOMEWHERE BENEATH CAIRO

TO: Initiates of the Twenty-First Nome
RE: Curses-in-Waiting

Initiates:

Welcome to Brooklyn House. I look forward to meeting you in person. Right now, though, I have to throw you in the deep end of the pool. Not Philip of Macedonia's pool – it's just a figure of speech, meaning I'm sending you on your first assignment.

I have inside-my-head knowledge that ~~Set~~ Murray, the god of evil, planted curses of annoyance throughout the Twenty-First Nome as payback for the Kane family's interference in his quest for world destruction. If unleashed one at a time, they would have only minor impact. But ~~Set being Set~~ Murray being Murray, he programmed them for simultaneous detonation on his next birthday – 29 December, the fourth Demon Day. If these magical ticking time bombs explode as planned, the level of irritation in your sector will immediately jump from moderate to extreme, resulting in anger-induced havoc.

Which brings me to your job: defuse the curses, and soon. My close association with ~~Set~~ Murray prevents me from using my own magic directly against his. But I've identified the known threats and outlined suggestions for neutralizing them. I'm nearly positive the solutions are legitimate. If not . . . well, try not to curse me too severely.

Threat: Foot-Traffic Jam

Harried pedestrians making their way through crowded hallways, corridors and pavements will suddenly find their way blocked by people sauntering, meandering or coming to a stop directly in front of them. The harried pedestrians will attempt to pass. They will fail. They will then try to shove through those blocking them. The blockers will take offence. Name-calling, chest-poking and other acts of righteous vexation will ensue.

Solution: Place the four Sons of Horus at the cardinal points around a likely target zone – a busy pavement at rush hour, for instance. Touch your wand to the main walkway within the zone and cast the dual spells of 'pass' (*faet*) and 'be at peace' (*ha-tep*).

The magic will branch like blue lightning through-out all the interconnected paths. The light will fade quickly, but the spells ensuring peaceful passage will remain in place.

Threat: Bump Her Cars

~~Set~~ Murray embedded storm magic in the tarmac of supermarket car parks. On his birthday, violent gusts will send shopping trolleys speeding into unsus-pecting vehicles. The resulting dents and scratches will infuriate the car owners, who will unleash words unfit for human ears. Slow-moving pedestrians may also be targeted by the wobbly-wheeled menaces. Those struck will likely suffer severe embarrassment with possible light bruising.

Solution: This curse can't be defused ahead of time, so action must be taken on ~~Set's~~ Murray's birthday itself. Distribute hippo, camel and vulture amulets to teams of initiates prior to sunrise. Fan out to potential curse hot spots. Hide with amulets at the ready. When a shopping trolley begins its death roll, crush it beneath a hippo or camel, or send it airborne via vulture. Note: all lion, cobra and crocodile amulets must be surrendered before returning home.

Threat: Opening and Closing of the Mouth

The sound of chewing is a hot button for many people. This curse uses a diabolical three-forked attack to magnify that irritation. First: the sounds of mastication will become juicier, stickier, crunchier and slurpier than normal. Second: the noises will be amplified tenfold. And third: the eaters will chew *with their mouths open*, offering a can't-unsee-that, seen-food visual. The usual mild level of exasperation will shoot up to Sekhmet-threat rage. And we all know where that can lead.

Solution: To prevent this curse, first summon water with the divine word *maw*. (Not to be confused with *mar*, the less-than-divine word for 'retch'.) Due to the vast quantity of liquid this word generates, I recommend standing in or near an empty bath. Enchant the water with a combination of the spells for 'silence' (*hah-ri*) and 'teeth' (*sinean*). Bottle the water in 100-millilitre recyclable containers and distribute them to the populace as free samples. With luck, you will reach enough people to minimize the testiness caused by open-mouthed chewing.

Threat: Oh, Poop

~~Set~~ Murray deposited hundreds of steamy piles of fresh dog poop throughout the Brooklyn area, then hid them with a combination *i'mun–n'dah* 'invisibility–protection' spell. Both spells will cease at precisely noon on his birthday, exposing the plops to the feet of unsuspecting passers-by.

Solution: Removing this curse will be potentially *mar-*inducing, so proceed with caution. Traverse the Twenty-First Nome on foot in two-person teams. As you walk, one person casts the divine word for 'reveal' (*sun-ah*) to expose the messes. The other follows with a 'clean' (*nidif*) spell. Note: to avoid becoming magically fatigued, bring a pooper-scooper and bags as backup to nidif.

MURRAY, YOU OLD DOG, YOU! ALWAYS AN INSPIRATION. I LOOK FORWARD TO SWAPPING EVIL STORIES WITH YOU WHEN I BECOME A GOD. IN THE MEANTIME I'VE PLANTED A LITTLE CURSE OF MY OWN THAT'LL DETONATE WHEN I DEPART BROOKLYN HOUSE FOR GOOD. – SETNE

THE QUIZ OF ISIS

Since Isis is the queen of divine words, I wondered if she ever used a special magic command, like abracadabra, to give her spells extra *oomph*. 'Why, yes,' Sadie dead-panned when I asked her. 'It's *flabbergasted*.' She was kidding, of course. I think.

True or False?

1. Isis is the goddess of wisdom.

    True   False

2. Isis is married to Osiris.

    True   False

3. Isis poisoned Ra.

    True   False

4. Isis saved Ra from poisoning.

      True   False

5. Isis reassembled Osiris after Set dismembered him.

      True   False

6. Isis's symbol is the *bau*.

      True   False

7. Isis's son is Anubis.

      True   False

8. Isis can only fly in kite (the bird, not the aerial toy on a string) form.

      True   False

9. Cleopatra VII was Isis's last host in ancient times.

      True   False

Answers:

1. **False.** Isis is the goddess of magic. As for being wise . . . well, let's just say she's made some questionable choices in her time, so maybe not.

2. **True,** though I want to be clear she's married to the *god* Osiris, not my dad, who is Osiris's host!

3. **True.** Isis wanted Osiris to be king of the gods. But Ra, her father, had the throne. So she set a snake on him that had venom with no known antidote. Like I said, she's made some questionable choices . . .

4. **True.** Surprise, surprise, there *was* an antidote, but only Isis knew it! She agreed to use it in exchange for Ra's ren, figuring that his secret name would give her power over him.

5. **True.** After curing him, Isis 'encouraged' Ra to give up the throne to Osiris. Set wanted the throne, though, so he sliced and diced his brother to bits. Isis put Osiris back together again, with her sister Nephthys's help. Probably the worst jigsaw puzzle ever.

6. **False.** A bau is an evil spirit and, while Isis might be conniving and power-hungry, she's not evil. Her symbol is the *tyet* knot, an emblem of protection.

7. **True, sort of.** She adopted Anubis after Nephthys gave him up.

Just realized how weird it would be for me to date Anubis if I was still hosting Isis! – Sadie

8. **False.** The kite is her sacred bird, but Isis can fly quite nicely thanks to her beautiful iridescent wings.
9. **Might be true, but possibly false.** Read my story about Horus and you'll understand.

THE MAGIC TOUCH
by Sadie Kane

When it comes to spells and divine words, no one beats Isis, goddess of magic. Back when I was her host, I had ready access to her vast knowledge. I still draw on her powers when I need to – that's the whole deal with the path of the gods, remember – but I've had to turn elsewhere to add to my magical library. Scrolls are a good source, and I can always portal-pop over to the First Nome to consult with Uncle Amos, the greatest living magician, or Duat-chat with the ba of Chief Lector Iskandar, the greatest dead magician.

Scrolls, Amos and Iskandar are rubbish, though, when it comes to channelling Isis in her goddess-of-motherhood mode. It's not an aspect of her power I tap into often, but now and then our youngest initiates – ankle-biters, as we call them, a name that is sometimes painfully accurate – need mothering. That's when I grab hold of my tyet amulet and reach out to my own mum, who, despite being a ghost, is the best mother I know. Plus, she has communed

81

with Isis, too, so I can get a double dose of maternal instincts from one source.

Recently I was in touch with Mum to seek advice about Shelby, our youngest and most powerful initiate. Here's how that conversation went:

ME: Mum! Mum! Mum! You there?

MUM: Yes, darling, I heard you the first time. How are you?

ME: Terrible. Shelby is driving me bonkers again.

MUM: What is it this time – lashing out with a *ha-wi* strike spell, or scaring people with crayon drawings that come to life?

ME: Worse. She went on a ha-di rampage. Destroyed her scrying bowl, her room, and then a good chunk of the fourth floor before I stopped her.

MUM: How *did* you stop her, may I ask?

ME: Um . . .

MUM: Oh, sweetie. You didn't bind her up with a tas spell, did you?

ME: I untied her right away. Well, almost right away. I just can't work out what set her off.

MUM: Hmm. She targeted her scrying bowl first? Had she been talking to anyone, do you know?

Quick interruption: scrying is an ancient method of communication whereby you huddle uncomfortably over a shallow bronze bowl filled with olive oil, ask to see someone or some place, then stare into the dish, hoping that the person or place appears. Inconvenient, unreliable and not at all mobile, scrying can literally be a pain in the neck.

ME: Shelby might have been talking to her parents. I heard they just had another baby.

MUM: Ah. That explains it.

ME: It does?

MUM: Sadie, Shelby is jealous. She's acting up to get attention. Carter did the same thing after you were born.

ME: He did? But I was so adorable! How could he not love me?

MUM: Obviously he came to love you. But at first he threw jealous fits, kicking and punching anyone and everything. Come to think of it, that should have told us that he'd be a good host for Horus.

ME: Kicking and punching I can deal with. Total destruction like Shelby's been doing . . . not so much. Any advice for dealing with her?

MUM: Try the magic touch. It helped me with Carter . . . and Isis with Horus.

ME: Yeah, you're going to have to explain that.

MUM: Right. Take a look at these.

At this point in the conversation, holographic images of Ancient Egyptian statues, stone carvings and tomb paintings appeared on my bedroom wall. Each of them showed a mother cradling her young son.

ME: Not you and Carter, clearly. Isis and Horus?

MUM: Yes. They look cosy, don't they?

ME: Never really thought of Isis as the cuddling type, but yeah.

MUM: Ah, yes, but these depictions don't tell the whole story.

Here, a new holographic image showing a little jackal-headed god replaced the ones of Horus and Isis. I swooned when I recognized the god.

ME: Swoon! Is that Anubis as a baby?

MUM: Yes, and please don't ever make that noise again. Anubis was Nephthys and Set's son, you remember, but Set rejected him. So, Isis and Osiris took him in. Well, Horus wasn't too keen on sharing his parents' attention. He puffed up into his avatar and threw a tantrum.

ME: Yikes. So, what did Isis do, punish him?

MUM: Quite the opposite. She went into avatar mode, too, and wrapped him in her arms. He fought against her embrace, but she held on tight, murmuring how much she loved him.

Eventually he listened. They resumed their normal forms. That's when cuddling took place.

Me: So the magic touch is the same as hugging it out.

Mum: Exactly. It worked for Isis; it worked for me. I think it could work for you, though you might want to call on Isis for a little extra hugging power with Shelby.

Me: Thanks, Mum. I'll give it a go tonight. Love you.

Mum: Love you, too.

In case you're curious, wrestling Shelby in a bear hug earned me a bruised rib. But it was totally worth it, because later, when I went to tuck her into bed, I found a picture she'd drawn of the two of us snuggled up together. And Shelby was smiling. So, mission accomplished – and additional destruction averted.

THE QUIZ OF NEPHTHYS

Nephthys is the goddess of rivers – specifically, the Nile. So it's surprising that she doesn't wield more power. I mean, the Egyptian civilization grew and thrived because of the Nile, right? And yet Nephthys takes a back seat to Set, Isis, Osiris and Ra. To me, that's as backwards as the Nile flowing from south to north.

> **Short answer essay question:** How does Nephthys feel about Set?
>
> Phew, this one's complicated! On the one hand, she loves him. I mean, she married him, so she must.

On the other hand, she's afraid of him, because, as the god of evil and violence, he can be violent and evil. He chopped up his own brother, Osiris, after all, and ripped out his nephew Horus's eye in battle. But for some reason Nephthys trusts that he won't hurt her, even though she defied him by helping Isis recover all of Osiris's body parts (ick). He also makes her sad. She had to give up their son Anubis because Set rejected him. So, I'm going to circle back to my original answer: Nephthys's feelings about Set are complicated!

THE MISSING PIECE
by Zia Rashid

A package came for me recently from the First Nome. Inside were a dozen *ostraca* – broken pottery pieces used by Ancient Egyptians for writing and drawing – and this note.

> Dear Zia,
>
> These arrived for you
> today from Makan al-Ramal
> al-Hamrah.
> May they bring you peace
> and understanding.
> Amos

Eleven of the potsherds were written in familiar handwriting – that of Chief Lector Iskandar. I teared up when I saw his script. History remembers him as the powerful leader of the House of Life, the magician who decreed that any mortal who hosted a god, willingly or unwillingly, would be put to death.

But to me he was a kind and gentle surrogate father. He rescued me after my village was destroyed. Years later, he saved me again, disobeying his own law and hiding me away when he discovered I was a godling.

The ostraca were his observations on the day Nephthys took me as her host. I say 'took' because I didn't know I was hosting her. Iskandar revealed her presence just before he secreted me away to the Place of Red Sands. There he placed us, goddess and godling, in a watery tomb shielded with magical protection.

Iskandar died while Nephthys and I slumbered together for three months. I never knew why he allowed her to remain merged with me – until now. As for Nephthys, I cannot pretend to know her the way I came to know Ra. These ostraca helped me to understand her a little better – especially the twelfth ostracon, which was written in a different hand. I'd never seen it before, yet it was as familiar as my own. I share all twelve now so that they may help you know her, and Iskandar, too.

Ostracon No. 1

Zia is different since her return from London.

Her yellow-red aura now flickers with blue, like the blue at the heart of a flame. What does it mean? Perhaps nothing more than that her skills with fire have intensified.

Ostracon No. 2

Our sau tells me that Zia asked him for a maw amulet. A fire elementalist wearing a water symbol is disturbing. If it was anyone else but Zia . . . Still, it would be prudent to watch her.

Ostracon No. 3

Zia is napping. I listen at her door. She is talking in her sleep. Hapi is happy. Why would she dream of the blue giant who inhabits the Nile?

Ostracon No. 4

I caught Zia staring at a memory in the Hall of Ages just now. A memory of Set screaming in anger at his wife's betrayal. When I pulled her back, her eyes were black with fear.

Ostracon No. 5

Zia lingers longingly by the fountain of Thoth,

plunging her arms deep in the water when she thinks I'm not looking.

Ostracon No. 6
Thoth help me, I have been blind. My fire child is the godling of Nephthys.

Ostracon No. 7
I have communed with the goddess. She has known from the start that Zia is not a suitable host. She can feel Zia's growing confusion. Yet the goddess hesitates to leave. She fears Set will discover her and force her to join him. Within Zia she is safe, her water hidden by Zia's fire.

Ostracon No. 8
Nephthys has a plan to save them both. She has promised to protect my fire child. Thoth help me, I pray it works.

Ostracon No. 9
My ancient hands shake as I sculpt. This, my last shabti, must be my masterpiece, every detail exact. More lives than Zia's depend upon it. But I confess her life is the only one I think of.

Ostracon No. 10

Zia knows. I needed a snip of her hair to imbue the shabti with her essence. She communes with the goddess even now.

Ostracon No. 11

The fear and trust in her eyes as I crossed Ra's crook and flail upon her chest . . . my heart breaks to remember it. Nephthys, preserve her sanity. Keep her safe. And free her at your first opportunity.

Ostracon No. 12

I found these potsherds scattered in the waters by our tomb. I send them with tears shed for your loss. May you meet Iskandar again in Aaru.

THE QUIZ OF HORUS

I'm not what you'd call buff or intimidating. (Keep your comments to yourself, Sadie!) **Oh, Carter, why would I say anything when your self-evaluation is so spot on? – Sadie** So, yeah, it was fun being the muscle while hosting Horus, the god of war. The downside to sharing my mind with him – apart from the constant threat of burning up when his power became too hot to handle – was having to listen to him brag about his victories. Funny how he never talked about his losses . . .

Circle the correct answer:

1. Horus's great-grandfather is a) Khufu;
   b) Imhotep; c) Ra; d) Tefnut.

2. What are the two different colours of
   Horus's eyes? a) baby blue and sea green;
   b) pitch black and milky white; c) gold and
   silver; d) it's a trick question – his eyes are
   swirling kaleidoscopes of all colours.

3. Horus's sword is called a a) *khopesh*;
   b) *wedjat*; c) *netjeri*; d) *tjesu heru*.

4. Horus has two sacred animals, one of
   which is mythological. What are they?
   a) penguin and sphinx; b) hippo and
   uraeus; c) cobra and serpopard;
   d) falcon and griffin.

5. Horus's avatar is a) penguin-headed hippo;
   b) a falcon-headed warrior; c) a flying cobra;
   d) an empty trench coat.

6. If Horus had a favourite toy, it would be
   a) Rock 'Em Sock 'Em Robots; b) a kite (the
   kind that flies on a string, not the bird);
   c) a hula hoop; d) a Paint the Tomb by
   Numbers kit.

Answers:

1. **c:** Khufu is the name of a famous pharaoh (also of our resident baboon). Imhotep was a famous architect, mathematician and healer. Teflon was . . . Wait, who was this again?

2. **c:** Thoth is the one with the kaleidoscope eyes.

3. **a:** The wedjat is Horus's hieroglyph symbol. A netjeri is a knife made of meteoric iron used during the Opening of the Mouth ceremony. The tjesu heru is a nasty two-headed snake.

4. **d:** Sphinx, uraeus and serpopard are all bizarre mythological creatures, though chances are an Ancient Egyptian would consider a penguin bizarre, too.

5. **b:** I've seen a flying cobra – called a uraeus – and an empty animated trench coat. But a penguin-headed hippo? C'mon, not even Egyptian creatures could get that weird.

6. **a:** Rock 'Em Sock 'Em Robots is a classic toy featuring two plastic robots that punch each other in the face over and over until one of their heads pops up. Pointless? Perhaps. Entertaining? Hugely. Would Horus have loved it? Definitely!

HORUS GETS IN TOUCH
WITH HIS FEMININE SIDE
by Carter Kane

J ust when you think you know a god, you discover
something new and surprising, as I found out on a
recent visit to the First Nome. Uncle Amos was
running late, so I wandered the Hall of Ages, the
miles-long corridor flanked by shimmering curtains
of memories from the ancient past to the present.
Each age has its own colour – gold for the dawn of
time, silver and copper for the height of Egypt's
power, blue for the years of Egypt's decline and fall to
Rome, red for the beginning of its modern history.
Our current era is deep purple.

I didn't hang out in purple – um, been there,
done that – and instead moved backwards in time.
Something between red and blue caught my eye. It's
not a good idea to dwell on the past, but I couldn't
stop myself. I entered the memory.

My mind exploded with images. I saw twenty-
year-old Cleopatra VII, the last pharaoh of Egypt,
spill out of a rolled-up rug and land at the feet of

Julius Caesar, a general of Rome. Her beauty captivated the fifty-two-year-old Roman, and the two became lovers. (I averted my eyes at that point.)

Twenty and fifty-two? I'm sorry, but *eww*! Although perhaps I'm not one to point fingers, since the boy I'm dating is sixteen going on five thousand. – Sadie

Time fast-forwarded one year to 47 BCE. Cleopatra gave birth to a baby she nicknamed Caesarion, or Little Caesar. She assumed that Caesar, who had no other sons of his own, would claim the boy. I sensed her triumph at the thought that one day her son would inherit Caesar's position and wealth as well as Egypt's throne.

Except he didn't. Caesar ignored Cleopatra's son and named his grand-nephew Octavian as his sole heir. Cleopatra's triumph morphed into rage. When Caesar was assassinated three years later and Octavian stepped into his grand-uncle's sandals, her rage twisted into an obsession to unseat Octavian and put Caesarion on the throne. But she couldn't do it alone. So, one night, with the toddler Caesarion at her side, she called for help.

'Isis!' Her demanding voice rang out in my mind. '*Isis!*'

The goddess of magic appeared. Cleopatra drew herself up. 'I offer myself as host.' Then she laid a hand on Caesarion. 'And I offer my son as host to your son.' Isis accepted and summoned Horus. They moved in that night.

I nearly pulled out of the memory then. The thought of a three-year-old toddler hosting the god of war – it was horrifying. Then I remembered how ferocious our own little ankle-biter Shelby could be. If Caesarion was anything like her, he probably held his own hosting Horus.

Then the memory sped forward. Cleopatra fell in love with Octavian's Roman rival, Mark Antony. She added her money, army and the power of Isis to his side. In 32 BCE, they challenged Octavian for control of Rome and Egypt. War raged for nearly two years. On 1 August 30 BCE Octavian won.

Devastated and humiliated, Antony committed suicide.

Ten days later, Cleopatra secluded herself in her bedroom. She removed a deadly asp from a basket and pressed its fangs to her chest. The asp bit her, pumping its poison into her veins. Asp venom doesn't kill instantly; it paralyses. Cleopatra collapsed on her bed and waited for death.

These scenes flashed through my mind at lightning speed. When the asp bared its fangs, though, they slowed, as if to show me something important. That's when I saw it – a dark red snake superimposed over the asp. I sucked in my breath.

The Chaos snake, Apophis!

No, I amended. *One of his minions.*

As though responding to my thoughts, the memory shifted again. I plunged deep into the abyss, where the cat goddess Bast was battling the serpent of Chaos. She faltered for a moment, just long enough for Apophis to dispatch his servant with a whispered order: *Strike Isis.*

The minion shot up through the Duat to Cleopatra's bedroom. It coiled around the asp. When the asp bit Cleopatra, the red snake bit Isis. Its poison mimicked the asp's venom. As Cleopatra succumbed to paralysis, so did Isis.

Isis once used a serpent to poison a VIG (Very Important God). That she was almost a victim of venom herself . . . well, karma, irony and all that. – Sadie

But unlike Cleopatra, Isis didn't want to perish. '*Horus!*'

Horus heard his mother's pleas. He deserted Caesarion, flew to Cleopatra's bedroom and wrenched Isis from the pharaoh's dying body. They fled south, away from Egypt and Rome and the magicians who, on Chief Lector Iskandar's orders, were banishing the gods. Using monuments, artefacts and temporary hosts like stepping stones, Horus and Isis reached a distant Nubian settlement called Kush.

I'd been to the ruins of Kush with my father. Now I was seeing it in its glory days. Kush wasn't as grand as Egypt, but it radiated power. At the centre of that power was the settlement's leader, an intelligent and ferocious warrior *kandake* named Amanirenas. **When Carter related this story to me, I thought he said, 'A warrior candy cane named Amana Radar Range.' – Sadie** A *female* warrior – *kandake* means *queen*. With her was her son, Prince Akinidad.

Horus appeared before them, the much-weakened Isis cradled in his arms. Amanirenas sized up the situation immediately. 'I offer myself as host,' she said. But, when Horus gestured for Isis to go to the queen, Amanirenas held up her hand. 'Not to her. To *you*.'

101

Isis protested. But Horus saw his chance for revenge. 'I will combine my strength with the kandake,' he told his mother. 'When she faces Octavian's forces – and she will – we will stop them together. I will fight to avenge Cleopatra, last of the pharaohs. I will fight for what Caesarion was denied. I will defeat them and deliver a blow to Octavian. And you will take the prince as your host, and heal while at my side.'

Prince Akinidad didn't seem too keen on hosting Isis, but Queen Amanirenas's eyes gleamed with triumph as Horus merged with her.

I didn't see what happened next, because Uncle Amos pulled me away from the curtain. Probably a good thing; I was getting a little too involved.

But later, back in the Brooklyn House library, I looked up Amanirenas and Akinidad. The queen did fight the Romans, just as Isis had predicted. She won, too, and took a bronze bust of Octavian – then known as Caesar Augustus, first emperor of the Roman Empire – as a trophy. She buried the bust in the ground beneath her temple door. For years to come, anyone who entered or exited stepped on his head.

Not a bad bit of revenge, Horus, I thought, knowing

that some Egyptian magic uses statues to affect people. Augustus probably had headaches for years.

I discovered other hints of Horus in Amanirenas's history, too. Like the fact that she lost an eye in battle; Horus had lost his left eye when fighting Set. Strabo, an Ancient Greek writer, described the kandake as having a 'masculine figure'. He could have been seeing Horus without realizing what he was seeing. And there's a stone etching depicting her as quite large and looming high above her foes. To me, the etching looks like Amanirenas is encased in Horus's avatar. A bird of prey, possibly a falcon, swoops overhead.

I also learned that Caesarion was killed by Octavian a mere eleven days after Cleopatra's death. That was sad, but not surprising. After all, he'd lost his mother and the god he'd hosted almost his whole life. That'd be enough to leave anyone vulnerable.

What did surprise me, though, was that Horus abandoned Caesarion to rescue Isis in the first place. I mean, Horus wasn't exactly the ideal son. He cut off Isis's head once just because she made him mad. But maybe saving her was his way of apologizing for that. And maybe it explains why he and I melded together so well. If I had been around when my mother's life was threatened, I would have given up anything to save her. Perhaps he recognized that side of himself in me.

Oh, and in case you're wondering, the idea of Horus being hosted by the fearsome warrior queen doesn't bother me. I like strong women. My mom is one. So is my girlfriend. And Sadie? She just might be the most powerful of them all.

Carter! I take back every mean thing I ever said about you! Which, I grant you, could take some time. It's a long list.

— Sadie

HORUS MERGED WITH A DAME, HUH? I GOT NO PROBLEM WITH THAT. SEE, I'VE GOT MY EYE ON A LITTLE DUAL-GENDER NUMBER MYSELF. I'D TELL YOU WHO, BUT THAT WOULD WRECK THE SURPRISE I HAVE IN STORE . . . — SETNE

THE QUIZ OF ANUBIS

I once asked Anubis how many funerals he had attended in his life. He gave me a strange look – though maybe it only seemed strange because he was peering at me through Walt's eyes. His reply was: 'All of them.'

Fill in the blanks:

1. Anubis is **my boyfriend.**

   While this is technically correct, given that Sadie is the one answering the questions, we were looking for *the god of funerals and death.*

2. You can recognize him by his **hotness. Also,**

his warm brown eyes, which he uses to melt my innards regularly.

> Again, though this is true enough in Sadie's case, the answer we were looking for is *jackal head.*

3. You are most likely to find Anubis **not in my bedroom! Honest!**

> Um . . . right. The answer is *in graveyards, at funerals, and any other place where death is present.*

For some reason, Carter gave up after this question. He didn't even get Walt to write anything about Anubis! Wonder why? – Sadie

OTHER
MAJOR
GODS
AND
GODDESSES

THE QUIZ OF BES

Three words: Best. Dwarf. Ever.

Short answer essay question: In ancient times, the magicians of the House of Life allowed Bes, the dwarf god, to remain in the mortal world when the other gods were banished. Was this a sound decision?

Absolutely! Bes is unique among the gods. For one thing, he doesn't take a host – at least, I don't think he does. I've never seen him as anything other than his wonderfully hideous self, anyway. Unlike some gods, who use humans for their own purposes, Bes is fiercely loyal to and protective of his mortal friends. He wouldn't hesitate to hurl his short, pot-bellied, Speedos-clad, hair-covered body in the path of danger to save someone he loves. And that sonic *Boo!* he blasts out of his enormous rubbery-lipped mouth has kept me alive more than once. If that isn't enough to convince you, ask anyone who's seen him with his girlfriend, Tawaret. No question in my mind: Bes is and always has been a class act deserving of special consideration.

GET UGLY
by Bes

Today's mortals mystify me. You're so obsessed with beauty that you ignore a source of real power. I'm talking about ugly, of course.

Before I go on, let me be clear. The ugly I'm referring to is on the *outside*. I'm not into *inside* ugly, and I don't associate with anyone who is. So, if you're reading this to get tips on hurling insults, belittling others to look bigger, or besmirching characters, the exit portal's over there.

Now, I know what you're thinking: *But, Bes, I have an adorable button nose, naturally tidy hair and perfect posture. How can I possibly channel the power of ugly?* Put your concern to bed, give it a kiss goodnight and turn out the light, because I have just the thing: my patented five-step uglification programme. And, yes, *uglification* is a word. Or perhaps you have a better term for the opposite of *beautification?*

Five Steps to an Uglier, More Powerful You!

Step 1: Put your best foot forward. Toenails make a statement, so don't be afraid to show them off! For the greatest visual impact, grow them out until they curl, then drag the tips across a rough, dirty surface until they are a ragged, filthy mess. If possible, contract a case of toenail fungus. Given enough time and neglect, the thick yellow crud will spread to all ten toes.

Sometimes it's not practical to go barefoot. Don't fret! Shoes, either on their own or paired with the right socks, can de-hance any look. Strut your stuff in Velcro sports sandals with black tube socks, or slip on a pair of Sobek's namesakes, Crocs, with or without plastic sparkle embellishments. Critics agree: they don't come any uglier than that! *Psst!* Bitten-down fingernails, dry, scaly

red hands and knitted fingerless gloves
are this winter's best-kept ugly secret.
Pass it on!

Step 2: Hair you go!
Nothing makes 'em run for cover like
body hair in all the right places. So, never
shave those legs and underarms. There's
power in your pits — go ahead and let
those rugs grow out into full shaggy glory!
And never wash them, either. Embrace
the musk! Also, over-productive facial
follicles are your friends, because no one
messes with a guy rocking an untrimmed
beard that merges with his eyebrows. Extra
points for sweater-thick back and chest
hair and curly nose and ear threads!
Psst! False beards are ancient history. But
false mutton chops are delish! And not
just for men any more. Pass it on!

Step 3: Get inspired by tired attire.
We've all been there – big night out and
nothing to wear. Well, you could wear
nothing, but I don't recommend it for

beginners. Instead, try these words on for size: fashion-faux-pas throwbacks. Mix and mismatch shoulder-padded jackets, bell-bottoms, belly shirts, mom jeans, prairie skirts and sailor shirts. Dig deep into history's closets for epaulettes, frilly neckwear, clogs and butt bustles. Or go for the never-fail look of a filthy, half-tied bathrobe over ill-fitting swimwear – baggy and droopy, or ultra-tight for the bulging-fat look: it's your choice! In the end, the only wrong way to look wrong is to look right. *Psst!* Beware the Hawaiian shirt. Once the go-to ugly garment, it's now worn 'ironically' by so-called cool people. Pass it on!

Step 4: Hair we go again!
Are you burdened with thick, manageable hair free of dandruff, split ends and knots? Don't despair. Solutions are as easy as tease, chop and tangle! To get the snarled effect, hold sections of hair upright and comb towards the scalp. Want to rock a no-maintenance do? Chop or

shave off random clumps with dull scissors or clippers, and avoid hair products. For a quick fix, insert gum deep into your tresses and knead thoroughly. And don't forget to top off your look with a gigantic multicoloured bow or slogan trucker cap! *Psst!* Never underestimate the stomach-turning power of lice. Pass it on!

Step 5: Express yourself.

If you find yourself in a troubling situation – chased by demons, say – remember: don't turn that frown upside down. Contort it into a scowl, a grimace or a snarl. Add a pair of crazy eyes; bug out both, or squeeze one shut for a glare that's sure to stop them in their tracks. But don't stop there. Flare your nostrils. Furrow your brow. Bare your teeth and gums. Loll out your tongue, shake your head and let the drool fly. Your facial expression will send your message loud and clear: I've got ugly on my side, so now *you're* the one in trouble!

Psst! Allow your pimples to thrive. Those little pus-filled bumps are wellsprings of power! Pass it on!

In conclusion, I'd like to leave you with one final word: *BOO!* My point? Ugly alone is strong. Ugly plus a good scare word bellowed in the face of an attacker is unstoppable. Don't worry if you haven't found your special word yet. Get ugly, and it will come to you.

Psst! Not sure if you're ready to go full-on ugly? Test-drive looks with unglamorous glamours! Pass it on!

Glamours are magical disguises that hide the true identity of a thing or person. Just thought you should know. – Sadie

THE QUIZ OF THOTH

Thoth is much more than just the god of wisdom. He invented writing, too, *and* came up with the idea for the House of Life. He's so in tune with the ibis that he appears with that bird's head when he's in god form. And don't even get me started on his special relationship with baboons . . .

Match the term from column A with a term from column B:

A	B
Djehuti	*A Short Treatise on the Evolution of Yaks*
Leechcraft	Tennessee and Egypt
Per Ankh	The form Thoth sometimes takes in the Duat
Sem priests	A known staining agent
Memphis	Ordinary magicians
Sphere of green gas	Thoth's actual Egyptian name
Barbecue sauce	Top-level magicians
Thoth's work in progress	The House of Life
Scribes	Not an area of study at the University of Memphis

Answers:

Djehuti: Thoth's actual Egyptian name. 'Thoth' came from the Greeks.

Leechcraft: Not an area of study at the University of Memphis. Neither is astrology, apparently.

Per Ankh: The House of Life.

Sem priests: Top-level magicians. Also, leaders of the 360 Nomes of the House of Life.

Memphis: Tennessee and Egypt. The US city is named after the one on Egypt. Or is it the other way round?

Sphere of green gas: The form Thoth sometimes takes in the Duat. Why? Because he's a little cray-cray, I think.

Barbecue sauce: A known staining agent. Also, delicious when applied to slow-roasted meat.

Thoth's work in progress: *A Short Treatise on the Evolution of Yaks*. Because . . . why?

Scribes: Ordinary magicians. Ordinary? I think not.

SPLISH SPLASH
by Cleo from Rio

I suppose I should have noticed the lab coat sooner. In my defence, the coat rack in the Brooklyn House library had a sizable collection of hoodies, sweatshirts and jackets left behind by our trainees. The grungy-looking lab jacket just blended in . . . until it didn't.

It's kind of a funny story how I found it, actually. I was dusting the scrolls in the library and thinking about the Book of Thoth – where it might be hidden, how I might get my hands on it, and what secret information about the deities it might contain. In fact, I was on the verge of commanding a retrieval shabti to find the book for me when a puff of dust hit my nose. I sneezed and . . . Okay, I admit it: I didn't cover my nose. Bogeys flew out.

That would have been the end of it, except my bogeys landed on the lab coat and the word *Gesundheit* lit up on the sleeve.

Now, I don't know about you – though, as a follower of Thoth, I'd *like* to know about you, because I like to know about everything – but the sudden appearance of that German word intrigued me. I stopped dusting and observed the coat from a safe distance.

After a few moments, the *Gesundheit* faded. The coat exhibited no further signs of illumination, but my Thoth senses were tingling. So, as an experiment, I inhaled some more dust and carefully sneezed on the coat again. This time, the words *Bless you* and *Agh* (Baboonese for 'good health') flashed like neon signs. Also, for some strange reason, the hieroglyphs for the god Shu.

My heart beat faster. Clearly, this was no ordinary barbecue-sauce-stained lab coat. I had a theory about who it belonged to, which I immediately put to the test.

'Fetch me the lab coat of the god Thoth!' I ordered the nearest retrieval shabti. The shabti came to life and hopped off its pedestal. It tossed the recently sneezed-upon garment to me, then surreptitiously wiped its clay hand on its clay leg and solidified back on its post.

So, there I was, holding the coat worn by my patron god when he was in mortal form. Since I was the only one at Brooklyn House following the path of Thoth, I logically concluded that it was a gift from him to me. With great reverence, I put it on and buttoned it up.

In hindsight, that wasn't a smart move. I'd barely fastened the last button when – *fwush!* – the coat lit up like the streets of Rio during Carnivale. It was as if the material had been storing data for months and couldn't wait to let it out. Words and hieroglyphs and numbers and symbols sparkled and glowed in dizzying hues of red, orange, blue, green, gold, purple and silver. I understood then why Thoth's eyes were swirling kaleidoscopes. My own felt like they were spinning out of my head as I plunged into the flashing, tie-dyed sea of information.

Somehow I maintained control and swam joyfully in that sea. But then the words and symbols started coming faster. They crashed over me like mounting waves, brighter and more complex, in every tongue imaginable and some unimagined. They flooded my senses. Overpowered, I stopped swimming and started drowning.

I struggled to take off the coat. The buttons wouldn't yield. My heart raced and my breathing shallowed. Then I couldn't breathe at all.

Suddenly a tiny voice spoke in my ear. 'Hey, come on. Relax, will you? Find your happy place before your head, like, literally explodes.'

I didn't recognize the voice. But when I heard it I remembered a story Sadie had told me, about how Carter had helped her change back from kite (the bird, not the flying toy) to human form by focusing on what was important in her life. **You see, Carter? I do give you credit sometimes. – Sadie** I squeezed my eyes shut and thought about my favourite beach, an isolated spit of sand on Ilha do Governador off the coast of my beloved Rio.

'Endless ocean,' I murmured, envisioning the words as I spoke them to increase their power. 'Waves washing over hot sand. The spray of the sea –'

Droplets of moisture hit my face. My eyes flew open. I tasted salt on my lips. *Sea* salt. I glanced at the lab coat. The fabric was blank except for the words I had uttered. The letters, blue-green tipped with white, spritzed seawater and sprinkled fine white sand onto the floor.

'*Nossa*,' I breathed in my native Portuguese. And it *was* cool, except for the mess it was making. The coat didn't unleash another flurry of words, thankfully, so I eased myself out of it. The spritzing and sprinkling ceased. I hung the coat on a hook, then headed out of the library in search of an animated mop and broom to clean up the puddles and sand piles.

When I reached the Great Room, I spotted Carter, Walt and Sadie huddled together at the foot of Thoth's statue. They were deep in conversation, so I held off on telling them what had happened. Instead, I gathered my cleaning supplies and returned to the library to tidy up.

But, to my puzzlement, the puddles had vanished. Where the seawater went, I don't know. And if you think not knowing doesn't bother me you're probably not a good candidate for following Thoth's path.

As for Thoth's coat, I've stowed it in a secure place in the Duat. Maybe someday I'll be ready for that amount of magic. For now, though, I'll stick to scrolls.

THERE I AM, MUCKING AROUND IN THE LIBRARY GIRL'S HEAD FOR INFO ON THE BOOK OF THOTH, WHEN — BOOM — HER BRAIN GOES INTO MAGIC OVERLOAD. SINCE I THOUGHT I MIGHT NEED THAT RESOURCE, I SNAP HER OUT OF IT WITH A LITTLE WHISPERED SUGGESTION.

TURNS OUT SHE DOESN'T KNOW DIDDLY ABOUT THE BOOK. BUT IT'S NOT A TOTAL WASHOUT, BECAUSE SHE'S GIVEN ME SOMETHING I NEED FOR MY SPELL. I HELP MYSELF AND EXIT, STAGE RIGHT. – SETNE

THE QUIZ OF NEITH

Sadie will tell you that I'm the last one to critique anyone's fashion sense . . . but come on – what is *up* with those two palm fronds Neith wears in her hair?

Circle the correct answer:
1. Neith is the goddess of a) hunting;
   b) weaving; c) bees; d) all of the above.
2. Neith's favourite weapons are a) macramé
   net traps; b) bow and arrows; c) time
   manipulation; d) all of the above.
3. Neith is obsessed with a) pockets;
   b) conspiracy theories; c) jelly babies;
   d) all of the above.

4. Neith will agree not to hunt you if you a) ask her nicely; b) offer her all your pockets; c) win at Rock, Papyrus, Scissors; d) none of the above.

Answers:

1. **d:** She is rather busy.

2. **d:** She is rather good at what she does.

3. **d:** She is rather crazy.

4. **d:** She is rather relentless. Advice: steer clear of her unless you are with a partner and you both have *shen* amulets!

GAMES NIGHT

Announcing Brooklyn House's First Ever
HOWL AT THE MOON Game Night

We're turning the Great Room into a Great Games Room! We'll play the games our ancestors played and make up our own rules if the real ones have been lost to the ages. We've got some great Brooklyn House originals, too, created by our very own trainees. It's guaranteed fun, with the added bonus of teaching you skills that could keep Khonsu the moon god from stealing your ren someday! So, come howl at him with us! Snacks provided!

SENET: This classic board game of sticks, chance and teamwork must have been a favourite, for it has been found in tombs and artwork throughout Ancient Egypt. Place your bets, throw the sticks and move your game pieces through the S-curve. If you get your tokens 'home' before your opponents, you win! And, yes, betting is required. Here at the Twenty-First Nome we play for custom-made amulets, courtesy of our expert sau, Walt Stone.

DOGS AND JACKALS: This exciting peg board game is also known as the Game of Fifty-eight Holes, because the board has fifty-eight holes. Two sides of twenty-nine each, to be exact. One player gets five dog-headed pegs, and the other gets five jackal-headed pegs. Roll a five to put a peg in play. (We use a dice, but in ancient times coins or sticks were likely used.) Get all five on the board and then hope for high rolls, because first one to get all five pegs to the end wins!

MEHEN: Yet another board game, but with a twist – a snaky twist, that is! The board is a slab of sandstone carved in the shape of a segmented, coiled serpent. The original game tokens have been lost, so we've borrowed some from a Monopoly game. The rules have been lost, too, so we made up our own. To play, you need an even number of teams. Half start their tokens by the serpent's head. The others start at the tail. Dice rolls determine how many segments you can move your piece. If pieces meet face-to-face, they have to wait until another token from their side catches up so they can 'overpower' their opponents together! First team to get all the tokens to the opposite end of the coil wins.

SHABTI CHARIOT CRASH: Everyone assumes the Greeks and Romans were the first charioteers, but archaeological evidence shows that the Egyptians used these two-wheeled wonders centuries earlier. This race – more of a melee, really – starts with chariot construction, using common household items such as toilet-paper tubes, ice-lolly sticks and empty tin cans. Then it's shabti-shaping time! Bring your own wax lumps (we'll have some on hand if you need extra) to form one horse and one driver. The first chariot to complete three laps around Thoth's statue wins. Crashing is encouraged, because it's more fun! Well, for spectators, anyway. Not sure how the shabti feel about it.

DUNG-BALL RACE: Every bit as disgusting as it sounds! Wind-up scarabs roll balls of dung, imported directly from Egypt, around a miniature racetrack. Winner takes all! (We've tried using real scarabs, but they don't make the journey from Egypt quite as successfully.)

THE QUIZ OF KHONSU

I hate it when there's a new moon. It makes me think that Khonsu has turned his back to me because he's up to no good.

Complete the sentences using the words from the list. *Note: not all words will be used!*

Word list:

Senet   moon   silver   Demon Days

clouds   crescent moon   ren   Nut   five

hot stuff   river   holidays   gamble   sheut

seven   sun   cheat   Apis Bull   time

Tefnut   sun disc

1. Khonsu is the god of the _____.
   His eyes are _____ and he wears an
   amulet in the shape of a _____.
2. He once played _____ with _____
   so she could earn extra days to give birth.
3. She won and earned _____days.
   These are called the _____.
4. Khonsu would love to _____ for
   your _____.
5. He thinks he's _____ but I think
   he's the hindquarters of an _____.

Answers:

1. Moon. Silver. Crescent moon.
2. Senet. Nut.
3. Five. Demon Days.
4. Gamble (we would also have accepted *cheat*). Ren.
5. Hot stuff. Apis Bull.

WHAT WAS THE POINT?

Egyptian magic uses words to channel the power of the gods. So you have to be careful about what you say and write. Usually we're on top of that here at Brooklyn House. But somehow this notice made it past us and onto the bulletin board in the training room. We all signed up, too, which means we all read it. And yet none of us picked up on the problem.

SIGN UP FOR TARGET PRACTICE!

Training Room, Monday Night,
Seven o'Clock Sharp

1. Jaz	7. Julian
2. Sean	8. Alyssa
3. Carter	9. Zia
4. Leonid	10. Shelby
5. Sadie	11. Cleo
6. Walt	

If you don't see it either, ask yourself this: what, exactly, is *target practice*? Do you shoot arrows or other projectiles at targets? Or are you practising to *be* the target?

The wording is troubling, to be sure. But what's even more troubling is that we're not 100 percent certain who posted the sign-up sheet in the first place. No one here is following the path of Neith, who seems the most likely deity to play a trick on us involving targets. According to Doughboy, whom I volunteered for surveillance, no one showed up for the practice. So, for now, it remains a mystery. But no worries. We'll figure out who did it, even if it means borrowing the Feather of Truth from Dad.

AH, WELL. MY ATTEMPT TO GET THEM ALL IN THE SAME PLACE AT THE SAME TIME SO I COULD ERADICATE THEM ALL AT ONCE DIDN'T WORK OUT. BUT, HEY, IT WAS WORTH A SHOT. GET IT? 'A SHOT'? I SWEAR, SOMEONE SHOULD BE WRITING THIS DOWN. – SETNE

THE QUIZ OF PTAH

I can't play Scrabble with Sadie any more. Ever since she met the creator god Ptah in that underground tomb in Bahariya, she has been making up words and passing them off as his. 'You're only challenging *ixyzqt* because it falls on a triple word score!' she insisted last time – *the* last time – we played.

True or False?

1. Ptah rocks the skinny beard.

    True   False

2. Ptah can open multiple portals per person.

    True   False

3. Ptah's hieroglyph symbol is a wad of spit.

    True   False

4. Ptah's favourite swear word is *Rats!*

    True   False

5. As a creator god, Ptah can create new things with a snap of his fingers.

    True   False

Answers:

1. **True.** Not many gods can wear pencil-thin chin hair, but he pulls it off.

2. **False.** One per customer only.

3. **False.** His symbol is the was, meaning power. His name does sound like someone spitting, though.

4. **Mm, maybe true.** He's been known to send hordes of rats on chewing and clawing rampages.

5. **False.** He creates by speaking words, which turn into objects. How else do you think the first banana or flamingo was made?

ICE, ICE BABY
by Felix Philip

Nobody believes there's a god of ice. But guess what? I just found out that the Nile froze twice – once in the year 829 CE, and again in 1010 CE. So, it could have happened in more ancient times, too, right? And if the Nile *did* freeze in olden days, then obviously a god had something to do with it, because deities were connected to all the important nature stuff: floods, earthquakes, death, sunshine, bugs that rolled poop into balls. Which means there *could* be an Egyptian god of ice!

I know what you're thinking: *But, Felix, no one's ever heard of an Egyptian ice deity!* Sure, there's no record of my ice guy, but he could still be real. There're *tons* of deities no one remembers or ever heard of. You know the name of the Egyptian sea god, for instance? Me neither, but I bet there is one, because Egypt runs smack into two seas, the Mediterranean and the Red.

Then there's all those blue-skinned gods. Blue represented the sky and water, right? But think what happens if you get super chilly. Your lips and skin turn blue! So maybe blue also stands for ice, and one of those blue gods is my ice guy.

If so, he wouldn't do *just* ice. Egypt isn't a super-cold climate, so he wouldn't have enough to do. But a lot of deities are in charge of more than one thing – funerals *and* death, magic *and* motherhood – so my blue god could make other frozen stuff, like ice cream and snow cones, on the side.

Which brings me to Ptah. He's blue. He's kind of been forgotten and has faded into the background behind Horus, Isis, Ra and the other big guys. And get this: he creates stuff just by uttering words he makes up. So maybe one day he happened to murmur the word *ice* – or *snow, slush, hail,* whatever – and *ka-bam!* The Nile freezes over and the Ancient Egyptians are making igloos next to the pyramids.

So, I've decided I'm going to follow the path of Ptah. He might not turn out to be my ice god, but from where I'm sitting, which is on the sofa surrounded by my penguins, he's the closest thing to it.

I DON'T KNOW ABOUT ANY GOD OF ICE. BUT A GOD OF THE SEA? YEAH, I THINK IT'S FAIR TO SAY I KNOW ABOUT THAT ONE. – SETNE

THE QUIZ OF APOPHIS

The other day Sadie joked that we should add snake charming to our curriculum. I know she was kidding, but I'm seriously considering it. Who knows? If Apophis rises up from the abyss again, maybe we can hypnotize him into submission. Anything would be better than having him explode all over the place.

> **Short answer essay question:** Can you imagine if the serpent of Chaos had been allergic to Bast?

> OMG! Spending millennia battling Ra's feline champion while sneezing? Priceless! Itchy, watery eyes and no hands to rub them with! If the agony

of having his tail trapped under the monument of Ma'at hadn't driven him insane, the constant sniffling from his stuffy nose would have. And then there's the scratchy throat, which would have been completely maddening, since his whole body is basically throat.

So, to answer the question . . . yes, I can imagine it.

And if you're wondering whether there's a story about Apophis in this book, there isn't. The less said about that snake, the better.

THE
ANIMAL
GODS
AND
GODDESSES

THE QUIZ OF THE ANIMAL GODS AND GODDESSES

I watched Shelby playing with her toys the other day. And by 'playing', I mean pulling the heads off her plastic animals and reattaching them to the bodies of headless dolls. (I'm afraid to ask where the dolls' heads are.) I wonder if the animal deities were created that way. It might explain why many of them are so cranky.

Match the deity's name to his/her corresponding animal, role and most noticeable attribute:

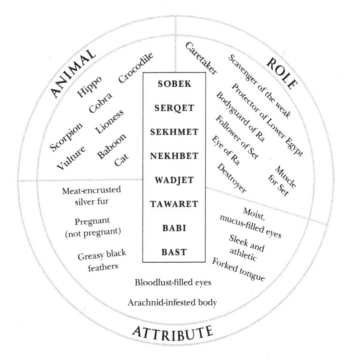

Sobek: Crocodile, Bodyguard of Ra, Moist,

    mucus-filled eyes

Serqet: Scorpion, Follower of Set,

    Arachnid-infested body

Sekhmet: Lioness, Destroyer, Bloodlust-filled eyes

Nekhbet: Vulture, Scavenger of the weak,

    Greasy black feathers

Wadjet: Cobra, Protector of Lower Egypt,

    Forked tongue

Tawaret: Hippo, Caretaker, Pregnant (not pregnant)

Babi: Baboon, Muscle for Set,

    Meat-encrusted silver fur

Bast: Cat, Eye of Ra, Sleek and athletic

ANIMAL SING-ALONG
by Tawaret

Like Bes, Tawaret is allowed to contact us now and then because, well, because she's the sweetest, most caring hippo you could ever hope to meet and she deserves to get whatever she wants. That last bit was in Bes's words, by the way, not mine. – Sadie

When Egypt was in its prime, I used to wallow in the Nile and listen to the youngest initiates of the First Nome learn this chant. It's silly, but it helped the little dears remember the river's animals – most of which are not silly but in fact quite deadly – and the gods and goddesses of those animals. The children did movements and made sounds to go with each creature, too. Best of all was the toe-tapping rhythm of the *sistrum* – that's an Ancient Egyptian rattle – and the drum. I simply had to shake my booty when I heard that *jingle-jingle tump-tump-tump*! Nephthys made me stop, though. She claimed my bouncy exuberance displaced too much of her river.

Back then, the chant went on for hours, because there were so many of us animal deities to sing about. Now, however, initiates only chant about the top eight. It breaks my heart how many of the old ones have been forgotten. When I think how much Heket, Gengen-Wer, Mekhet and the rest of the darlings here at Sunny Acres would enjoy hearing children chant their names . . . Well, maybe someday.

ZIA LEARNED THE EIGHT-ANIMAL CHANT WHEN SHE WAS AT THE FIRST NOME. SHE TAUGHT IT TO THE ANKLE-BITERS AT BROOKLYN HOUSE. SHE REFUSED TO DO THE MOVEMENTS, THOUGH. I ASKED IF IT WAS BECAUSE THEY COMPLETED A DANGEROUS MAGIC SPELL WHEN DONE WITH THE CHANT AND THE MUSIC. TURNS OUT THEY'RE JUST EMBARRASSING – AS CARTER DISCOVERED WHEN I CAUGHT HIM PRACTISING THEM IN HIS ROOM.
– SADIE

*(Arms straight out, palms together; open and close like
a crocodile mouth on chomp)*

Deep in the Nile lurks a crocodile
Sobek (*chomp-chomp*), Sobek (*chomp*)

*(Stand on tiptoe and lumber forward,
arms doggy-paddling)*

Nearby is a hippo, swimming on tiptoe
Tawaret (*splash-splash*), Tawaret (*splash*)

(Bare teeth and circle head around while roaring)

A lioness roars on the sandy shores
Sekhmet (*roar-roar*), Sekhmet (*roar*)

*(Alternate pats to the rump – your own rump,
please – while barking)*

While a bright-bummed baboon barks out of tune
Babi (*agh-agh*), Babi (*agh*)

*(Circle the room flapping and cawing; if desired,
one child can play the 'victim')*

A vulture flies while its victim dies
Nekhbet (*caw-caw*), Nekhbet (*caw*)

*(Curl first two fingers of right hand in front of mouth
and jab forward while hissing)*

Fangs don't miss in the cobra's kiss
Wadjet (*hissss-hissss*), Wadjet (*hissss*)

*(Raise arm over head, shape thumb and middle finger
in a sideways C and dart forward)*

The scorpion's sting could mean the end of things
Serqet (*zztt-zztt*), Serqet (*zztt*)

(Wiggle bum and pounce)

But the cat saves the day in a *purr*-fect way!
Bast (*meow-meow*), Bast (*meow*)

SUNU, HEAL THYSELF
by Jaz

Magic should come with a warning label: *Can be hazardous to your health. Side effects include dizziness, extreme fatigue and blackouts. Prolonged exposure has been linked to spontaneous combustion and addiction to unlimited power.* And that's just the stuff we know about.

Given how dangerous magic is, you'd think I'd be overrun with patients in need of my *sunu* healing talents. But after we won the battle against Chaos my workload was very light. It was frustrating, because in order to expand my knowledge I needed new cases to treat. So I took matters into my own hands.

Don't misunderstand me. I didn't run around inflicting pain, sickness and magical infections on the residents of Brooklyn House. No indeed! I inflicted them on myself.

I took it slow at first – a papyrus cut here, a patch of scaly (as in reptilian) skin there, a purple-and-orange rash everywhere. A bandage, a salve and an ointment took care of them easily. So I moved on to more challenging problems that required spells and magical medication: deviating and then undeviating my septum, growing hair where hair shouldn't be and then pruning it back (Bes asked for the instructions for this affliction, but not the cure) and the dreaded belly-button reversal (innies become outies, and vice versa). Again, great results, no side effects.

I was on a roll and . . . Okay, I'll admit it. I got overconfident. So, I threw a real doozy of a malignancy at myself – the Tongue Twister. This ailment is as rare as it is painful. The only known cure is an incredibly complicated spell that must be chanted with absolute precision. I was the only sunu capable of speaking the spell. The trouble was that I had given myself the Tongue Twister, which, as the name implies, twists the tongue. In short, the power of clear speech was no longer in my wheelhouse.

Frantic, I grabbed the spell and ran to find Sadie. She isn't a healer, but she was the best spell-caster I knew. If she could just loosen my tongue a little bit, I could manage the rest.

I found her in the Great Room by the statue of Thoth, talking to Carter and Walt.

'Bleah-glup!' I yelped. '*Bleah-glup!*'

'And a very *bleah-glup* to you too, Jaz,' Sadie replied politely.

'Is that a Nashville cheerleader word or something?' Walt wondered.

Sadie shrugged. 'Search me. I'm not a cheer-leader. I *get* cheered for.'

'Or booed at,' Carter put in.

'*Srrdimm,*' I growled in frustration. '*Fffffttzzzzttt!*'

Walt's eyes widened with alarm. 'Good Ra, she's sprung a leak.'

'*Pa-pa-pa-pa-GORP!*'

'Whoa, steady there, Jaz,' Sadie said, holding her hands up defensively. 'No need to get all hot under the collar!'

'Hold up,' Carter said. 'I think she really *is* getting hot under the collar!'

My hand flew to my throat. They peered at my neckline and exchanged worried looks. 'Uh-oh. The power of Sekhmet is coming through,' Walt muttered. 'We need to find out what's wrong. *Now.*'

Their worry morphed to fear, and with good reason. Sekhmet wasn't called the Destroyer for nothing. If I was channelling that part of her magic . . .

I roared – or tried to. It came out as a squeaky, high '*Eeee-blblblblbl!*'

'Jaz!' Sadie cried in horror. 'Your tongue! It's all twisted! Is that why you can't talk correctly?'

I nodded vigorously.

'Who did this to you?' Carter demanded.

I hung my head and pointed to my chest.

Sadie looked grim. 'Her shirt. Her shirt did it.'

'No,' Walt objected. 'I think she did it to herself. And she can't cure the problem because she has to speak a spell. Right?'

Nodding again, I handed Sadie the spell and pleaded to her with my eyes. She looked at the papyrus and whistled. 'This is a toughie. If I get even one word wrong, I could make things even worse. Maybe you should wait for it to wear off?'

I blinked back tears and shook my head.

Sadie took a deep breath. 'Okay. I'll give it a try. Let's – '

Before she could finish, Khufu intervened. He'd been watching and listening from his perch on Thoth's head. Now he dropped down, snatched the scroll from Sadie and shoved it into his mouth.

'Khufu! No!' Sadie cried. 'Bad baboon! Bad!'

Khufu rolled his eyes, spat out the papyrus, jumped up and shoved it into *my* mouth. If you're ever given the chance to taste papyrus infused with

151

baboon saliva . . . don't. I gagged and started to spit it out, but Khufu slapped his paw over my mouth. That left just one way to get the foul taste out of my mouth: chew and swallow. So, that's what I did.

Khufu removed his paw with a satisfied grunt and padded away.

'*Uh*, gross!' I yelled. 'Somebody get me a toothbrush!'

Khufu's technique had worked!

Walt, Carter and Sadie stared at me and then started laughing. 'Remind me never to bother reciting spells again,' Sadie said. 'I'll just eat them instead.'

'Not me,' I said. 'Now, if you'll excuse me . . . Somewhere in this house there's a bottle of mouthwash with my name on it.'

THE QUIZ OF BAST
by Sadie Kane

I once made the mistake of telling Bast that I'd wished I had a dog when I was younger. She just stared at me. I now understand the phrase 'If looks could kill . . .' – Sadie

Circle the correct answer:

1. Bast once had a crush on a) Apophis;
   b) Bes; c) Ra; d) none of the above.
2. Bast conceals weapons in her a) sleeves;
   b) puffed-up hair; c) amulet; d) enemies'
   bodies.
3. Bast is afraid of a) nothing; b) Tawaret;
   c) Horus; d) yarn.

4. Bast taught two classes at Brooklyn House. What were they? a) Shedding and Yowl for Attention; b) Glaring and You CAN Hack Up That Hairball!; c) Napping and Advanced Cat Grooming; d) Cardboard Box Sitting for Beginners and I Brought You This Dead Mouse.

5. Bast is also known as a) the Fart of Camel; b) the Eye of Ra; c) the Claw of Shredding; d) the Can of Whiskas.

Answers:

1. **d:** The cat goddess does not have crushes on others. She does, however, allow others to have crushes on her while she pointedly ignores them.

2. **a:** And by weapons we mean wickedly sharp knives that she deploys by flicking her wrists. FYI: her puffed-up hair indicates that something has scared her. When she's scared she's likely to flick her wrists, so steer clear! She wears an amulet on a collar, but it isn't a weapon. (At least, I don't *think* it is.) Change the word *conceals* to *jabs, stabs* or *buries*, and the correct answer would be *d*.

154

3. **b:** Tawaret is a gentle giant unless her squeeze, Bes, is harmed in any way. Since Bast once toyed with Bes's affections like . . . well, like a cat with a mouse, she learned to stay out of Tawaret's way. As for the others, I bet she could take Horus in a fight, and I've seen her go ballistic on a ball of yarn.

4. **c:** I must talk to Carter about adding Yowl for Attention and Glaring to our curriculum. I would be excellent at teaching both.

5. **b:** Do cats even fart? I know they shred, and look out when there's a can of Whiskas being opened! But of course the answer is the Eye of Ra. Bast was Ra's champion, battling Apophis, the serpent of Chaos, for thousands of years deep in the abyss.

MUFFIN TO THE RESCUE
by Sadie Kane

Not long after saving the world from the forces of Chaos, I received a package from Gran and Gramps Faust. Inside was a jumble of belongings I'd left behind in London, a tin of Gran's famous burnt biscuits (*cookies*, you Americans call them) and this note:

> Dear Sadie,
>
> Heard that barmy baboon god and nutter vulture goddess are back in the Duat where they belong. Good riddance. Why they ever thought Gran and I would make compatible hosts is beyond me. Took us weeks to clean up their mess — with no help from the House, of course. Damn magicians are never around when you need them, only when they need you.
>
> Gran says to return the biscuit tin.
>
> Gramps

Such a heartfelt outpouring of emotion for their only granddaughter. Still, they're wonderful in their own quirky way. I quite love them, and I know that they love me.

After I'd read the note and introduced the biscuits to the nearest rubbish bin, I rummaged through the box. Among the bits and bobs was an old cassette tape. Carter and I have recorded messages on such tapes (maybe you've read the transcripts?), but this wasn't one of those. Curious, I popped it into my old tape recorder and hit PLAY.

Mrow.

My jaw dropped at Muffin's distinct meow, because honestly, in the six years she was my cat, I never once suspected she knew how to use a tape recorder. Oh, or that she was the cat goddess Bast. But seriously the tape-recorder thing blew me away.

I'd like to say the recording blew me away, too, but it was just a lot of meowing and purring, plus one unfortunate hairball incident that sounded as disgusting on tape as it would in person. I don't speak Cat, but I remembered a divine word Uncle Amos had once spoken to communicate with our Russian friend, Leonid. I figured it was worth a shot, so I held the tape and murmured, '*Med-wah.*' Speak.

157

Suddenly Bast's voice filled the room. Other voices, too, but mostly Bast's. I choked up a little, hearing her. But as I listened I started to smile because . . . well, it was just so *Bast.*

That's when I realized the recording was a gold mine for trainees who might follow the path of the cat goddess. So I woke up Doughboy – the ill-tempered wax shabti from my dad's magic kit – and instructed him to transcribe it onto papyrus. I've entitled it *The Book of Being Muffin*, because . . . well, read the highlights below and you'll see why.

FROM *THE BOOK OF BEING MUFFIN*

ON TRANSPORTATION

Julius, I shall be forever indebted to you and Ruby for releasing me from the prison abyss. But if you ever cram me inside that infernal cat carrier again I will claw my way up one side of your body and down the other.

ON NAPPING

It's only been a month since I burst out of an Ancient Egyptian obelisk and landed inside this orange tabby cat. Yet in that short time I have become brilliant at napping.

ON SHREDDING

MUFFIN: Ha-ha! Take that, cursed flowered upholstery!

GRAMPS: *Agh!* Gerroff, cat!

ON SEAFOOD-FLAVOURED WHISKAS

[Sound of Sadie opening a can of Whiskas]

SADIE: There you go, Muffin.

[Silence]

SADIE: Come on, eat up. It's chicken. You like chicken.

[Silence]

SADIE: Suddenly you don't like chicken. Well, I'm *not* giving you a different flavour.

[Silence]

SADIE: Stare all you want. I won't cave.

[Silence]

SADIE: Fine.

[Sound of Sadie opening a second can of Whiskas]

MUFFIN: Works every time.

ON THREATS

My chief mission is to protect my kitten, Sadie. Danger lurks in every room. So far, I have subdued a brown paper bag in the living room by repeatedly diving inside, rustling about and charging out. In the kitchen, I conquered a balled-up bit of foil by ignoring it for a full minute and then pouncing. It is now in the abyss beneath the refrigerator. Nothing ever returns from that dark place. I also ferreted out a cup of tea that tried to hide on the counter. Then Gran weighed in and finished the job, dispatching the remains before they could reassemble for a counterattack.

To date, only one enemy has eluded me. The mysterious red dot appeared out of nowhere and darted about Sadie's room at random. It survived multiple direct paw hits, then vanished. It escaped this time, but be warned, dot . . . I will not fail again.

I remember this. The dot was the light from Liz's laser pointer. It was probably mean of us to keep flashing it around the room, but . . . gods of Egypt, we laughed so hard watching Muffin chase it!

ON BEING WITH SADIE

SADIE: Muffin, why must you always sleep on my head?

MUFFIN: If I didn't, your ba might take flight.

She might have been right, actually. Whenever I slept over at Liz's and Emma's houses, I had disturbing dreams about flying. I realize now that those dreams were my ba leaving my body. I never had them when Muffin snuggled on my head.

SADIE: Muffin, do you have to stare while I practise my dance moves?

MUFFIN: Dance? I thought a demon had taken possession of your body.

I don't know what she meant by that. My moves were fierce.

SADIE: Muffin, do you think Dad and Carter ever miss me?

For some reason the med-wah spell didn't translate Muffin's soft meow and gentle purrs here. Maybe because the sounds spoke for themselves.

THE BIG REVEAL
by Setne

Well, this *has* been fun, folks. But I've gotta get going. See, tonight's the night I say buh-bye to my death as a ghost and howdy to my life as a god. Oh, yes, you heard right. While you were busy reading this book, I was gathering everything I need for my showstopping transformation. A boat with a demonic captain, summoned from the Duat to sail me though the River of Night? Check. The djed amulet, symbol of rebirth, stolen from Carter's locker? Check. Seawater, conjured from the surf of a distant island? Check.

Oh, by the way, I've been dying to point out the happy coincidence of that island's name, Ilha do Governador! It means Governor's Island, my friends, the same name as the plastic world within my snowglobe prison. Names have great power, right? So, with a little sympathetic magic razzle-dazzle, I'll use that cursed globe to take over the island. But I won't destroy the Ilha do Governador. Oh, no. The island will become my oasis, the seat of my power, the place where I can see and command my vast realm.

But, Setne, you ask, *how is all this possible?* The

Book of Thoth, of course. Yes, I found it at last, tucked underneath my one-time prison, of all the stupid places. But it is mine now. Its secrets are mine. Its magic is mine. The ultimate spell of transformation – *mine.*

And so tonight I will hook up with my old pal Bloodstained Blade. We'll sail the River. Towards journey's end I'll get out the Book of Thoth and begin chanting the spell. When the light is just right – that purple-gray shade of predawn – I'll drop the djed amulet into the seawater. A little more chanting, and the water will turn a magical blue-green. Then, as my boat emerges to greet the first rays of Ra, I'll pour that water over my head.

Guess what happens next? Oh, you never will, so I'll tell you.

I will be reborn as Wadj-wer, the Great Blue-Green, the long-lost, long-forgotten, always-overlooked Egyptian god of the sea! Also – and this is a terrific bonus, I gotta say – the *goddess* of fertility. It's the two-for-one immortality deal of the millennium! With his power, I will take over the oceans. With her power, I will repopulate the world.

So get ready. Tomorrow morning there'll be a new god in town. And he is me.

GET REKHET
by Walt Stone/Anubis

Yeah, none of that stuff Setne outlined ever happened. Carter, Zia, Sadie and I were on to him the whole time. Let me explain.

Setne's a slippery dude, so we knew he'd break out of his snow globe eventually. We also knew it would be bad if he sneaked out without us noticing. So we orchestrated the timing of his escape by literally cracking open his prison door. **I'm a little offended Setne thought I'd miscast my sahad-w'peh. As if I'd be that careless! – Sadie**

Once he was out, I took charge of tracking his activities. As the god of death, I can see ghosts even when they're invisible. Either Setne forgot that, or he wildly underestimated Walt's death magic, because he moved around as if he owned Brooklyn House. The trapdoor, the supply cupboard, the basketball court, the library, a few bedrooms – he checked out everything. **Oh, gods, tell me my bedroom wasn't one of them! Ick, ick and triple ick! – Sadie**

He took a few trips off campus, too. He came back from the Needle vibrating with power, but luckily used up most of that energy digging around in Cleo's brain. **Mmm, not sure Cleo found that lucky. She had headaches for days afterwards. – Sadie** I almost lost him on his visit to the Duat to find Bloodstained Blade. He returned, though, no doubt because he suspected that the Book of Thoth was somewhere in Brooklyn House.

He was right about that, and about the book being hidden in plain sight. But he was wrong about finding it. The book underneath his snow globe was called *The History of Pavement,* on loan from a friend of Carter's from Long Island and hidden beneath a glamour to look like the Book of Thoth. The real Book of Thoth is in the hands of the god who wrote it. If you want to see it, take a look at the papyrus the statue of Thoth is holding. Don't wait too long, though. We'll be moving it to a more secure location soon.

Speaking of secure locations . . . remember the mysterious mastaba with the sealed trapdoor? Well, one of the perks of hosting Anubis is unlimited free travel to places of death. I popped down, had a look around to make sure there were no nasties lurking about (there weren't), then impressed my girlfriend by reversing the magic that kept the trapdoor shut and opening it from the underside.

Just don't plan on visiting the mastaba anytime soon. It's being haunted by a new ghost – Setne. Multiple containment spells plus a double tas binding of the Seven Ribbons of Hathor, courtesy of Zia and Shelby (that ankle-biter's power is truly terrifying), should hold that 'slimy git', as Sadie would call him, until Osiris sends for him.

If Setne complains, I'll find him new quarters. I saw a musical snow globe among the junk Gran and Gramps sent. It should do quite nicely – especially because it plays 'The Chicken Dance' (rated one of the most annoying songs of all time by me) over and over and over again. – Sadie

A FINAL WORD

Agh!

TRANSLATION: You've reached the end of the book. Why are you still reading? Close it and go and play basketball, will you? – Khufu

ABOUT THE MAGICIANS
(IN ORDER OF APPEARANCE)

KHUFU – Not technically a magician because he's not human, Brooklyn House's resident baboon can do some magic, such as portal-opening, healing and communing with gods and animals. He has golden fur, a vibrantly coloured bum and wears a Los Angeles Lakers jersey.

CARTER KANE – The older Kane sibling. He has dark curly hair and dark-brown eyes. He once hosted the god Horus and now follows this god's path. His speciality is combat magic. He was crowned pharaoh of Egypt but chooses to teach magicians-in-training rather than rule.

SADIE KANE – The younger Kane sibling, this former host of the goddess Isis has blue eyes and blonde hair with a dyed streak of varying colours. A powerful magician, her abilities include spell casting and opening portals. She is following the path of Isis.

JULIUS KANE/OSIRIS – Carter and Sadie's father, Ruby's husband, and Amos's older brother. He sacrificed himself to become the host of the god Osiris. As Julius, he's muscular, with a shaved head and goatee, dark-brown skin and brown eyes, and wears well-tailored suits. As Osiris, he's blue-skinned but equally muscular and wears a traditional Egyptian kilt, neckbands and jewels of the god of the Underworld.

RUBY KANE – Sadie and Carter's mother, Julius's wife, and daughter of Gran and Gramps Faust. Blonde-haired and blue-eyed like Sadie and a powerful diviner, she died while releasing the cat goddess Bast from the prison abyss. She wears jeans and a T-shirt with an ankh symbol.

ZIA RASHID – A powerful fire elementalist, she has hosted two deities, Ra and Nephthys. Her straight dark hair frames her olive-hued face, dark eyes and full lips. She is following the path of Ra.

WALT STONE/ANUBIS – Walt died from King Tut's death curse but lives on as the host of the god Anubis. As Walt, he's good-looking and muscular, with a clean-shaven head and medium-brown skin and wears athletic clothing. As Anubis, he has warm-brown eyes, a pale complexion and tousled black hair, and wears

169

either a T-shirt and jeans with a biker jacket or a traditional Egyptian kilt and a ruby collar. He sometimes appears in his jackal-headed form. Walt/ Anubis is a top-notch death magician and highly skilled sau (charm-maker).

SETNE – The son of the Ancient Egyptian pharaoh Ramesses II, this evil, manipulative magician stirred up trouble when he was alive and is even worse now that he's a ghost. Short and scrawny, with greasy black hair, a hawkish nose, thin lips and black eyes, he wears skinny jeans, T-shirts, jackets with padded shoulders and lots of gold jewellery. Also known as Prince Khaemwaset.

AMOS KANE – Sadie and Carter's uncle, Julius's younger brother, former host of the god Set, and current Chief Lector of the House of Life. Barrel-chested, with dark skin and dark hair in cornrows braided with gems. He wears round glasses, stylish pinstripe suits and the traditional leopard-skin cloak of the Chief Lector. He is following the path of Set.

Doughboy – Not a magician but rather a shabti that originally belonged to Julius Kane. Now under Sadie and Carter's control.

Bloodstained Blade – A demon with the head of a double-bladed axe, he was bound in servitude to the Kane family as the captain of their boat, the *Egyptian Queen.*

Leonid from St Petersburg, Russia – A Russian-born teenage magician with enormous ears. He speaks broken English and wears a tattered military uniform. He is following the path of the god Shu.

Iskandar – A two-thousand-year-old magician with light-brown wrinkled skin and milky eyes, he rescued Zia Rashid when her village was destroyed. The former Chief Lector of the House of Life, he imposed the ancient law that banished the deities deep into the Duat. He died shortly after meeting Carter and Sadie. He currently guards the Gates of the West as a ba.

Disturber – A minor blue-skinned and ancient-looking god of the Underworld, he assists the god Osiris.

VLADIMIR MENSHIKOV – An evil magician who plotted to release Apophis from his prison and then host the Chaos serpent. Now deceased, he wore a white suit and also white sunglasses to cover his eyes, which had been ruined when a spell backfired in his face.

CLEO FROM RIO DE JANEIRO, BRAZIL – Brooklyn House's brown-haired librarian-magician, she is fluent in many languages and a valuable researcher. She is following the path of Thoth.

FELIX PHILIP – A tween magician with a love of penguins, he hopes to discover the Egyptian god of ice. In the meantime he's following the path of Ptah.

SHELBY – The youngest resident of Brooklyn House, this kindergartener – aka 'ankle-biter' – has astonishing magical powers.

JAZ FROM NASHVILLE, TENNESSEE – A blonde-haired teenage magician and former cheerleader. Brooklyn House's skilled sunu, or healer, she follows the path of the goddess Sekhmet.

Glyphs and Spells

 DROWAH – boundary

 FAET – pass

FLABBERGASTED

 HA-DI – destroy

 HAH-RI – silence

 HA-TEP – be at peace

 **HA-WI** – strike

 **HI-NEHM** – join

 I'MUN – hide

 MAR – retch

 MAW – water

 **MED-WAH** – speak

 **N'DAH** – protection

 **NIDIF** – clean

SAHAD – unlock

 **SINEAN** – teeth

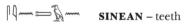 **SUN-AH** – reveal

 **TAS** – bind

GLOSSARY

AARU – paradise

ANKH – hieroglyph for *life*

BA – one of five parts of the soul; the personality

BAU – an evil spirit

BENNU – phoenix

CHIEF LECTOR – the leader of the House of Life

DEMOTIC SCRIPT – an informal system of Ancient Egyptian writing

DJED – a hieroglyph that stands for stability, strength and the power of Osiris; also symbolizes Osiris's rebirth

DUAT – a magical realm that coexists with our world

GLAMOUR – a magical disguise

GODLING – a person who is hosting a god or goddess

HIERATIC SCRIPT – a system of Ancient Egyptian writing similar to hieroglyphs, only less formal

HIEROGLYPHICS – a writing system of Ancient Egypt, which used symbols or pictures to denote objects, concepts or sounds

IB – one of the five parts of the soul; the heart

ISFET – chaos

KA – one of the five parts of the soul; the life force

KANDAKE – a warrior queen

KHOPESH – a sword with a hook-shaped blade

MA'AT – order of the universe

MASTABA – an Ancient Egyptian tomb with a flat roof and sloping sides

MEHEN – an ancient game with a board shaped like a coiled snake

MENHED – a scribe's palette

NETJERI BLADE – a knife made of meteoric iron used for the Opening of the Mouth ceremony

NOME – district, region

OSTRACON (pl., *ostraca*) – broken pieces of pottery used for writing and drawing

PER ANKH – the House of Life

PHARAOH – a ruler of Ancient Egypt

REKHET – a magician who specializes in healing magic

REN – one of five parts of the soul; the secret name, identity

SAHLAB – a warm Egyptian drink

SARCOPHAGUS – a stone coffin, often decorated with sculpture and inscriptions

SAU – a charm maker

SCARAB – a beetle known for rolling its dung in a ball

SCRIBE – a magician

SEM PRIEST – an experienced, upper-level magician

SENET – an ancient board game that involves gambling

SERPOPARD – a mythical animal with a long neck

SET ANIMAL – a mythical animal that looks like a dog with cone-shaped ears; a creature of Set, the god of evil

SHABTI – a magical figurine made out of clay or wax

SHEN – eternal; eternity

SHEUT – one of the five parts of the soul; the shadow

SISTRUM – a bronze noisemaker

SUNU – a healer

TJESU HERU – a snake with two heads – one on its tail – and dragon legs

TYET – a magic knot and the symbol of Isis

URAEUS – a winged snake

WAS – power; staff

WEDJAT – the Eye of Horus; a symbol of power and health

HIEROGLYPH KEY

A	B	C	D	E	F	G
H	I	J	K	L	M	N
O	P	Q	R	S	T	U
V	W	X	Y	Z	KEY	

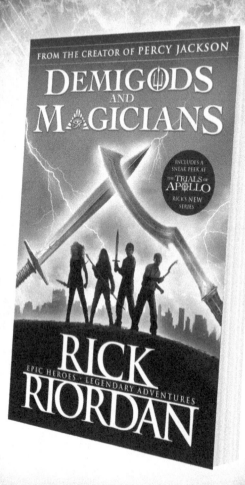

THE ADVENTURE NEVER STOPS . . .

PERCY JACKSON

THE GREEK GODS ARE ALIVE AND KICKING!

They still fall in love with mortals and bear children with immortal blood in their veins. When Percy Jackson learns he's the son of Poseidon, god of the sea, he must travel to Camp Half-Blood – a secret base dedicated to the training of young demigods.

PERCY JACKSON AND THE LIGHTNING THIEF
PERCY JACKSON AND THE SEA OF MONSTERS
PERCY JACKSON AND THE TITAN'S CURSE
PERCY JACKSON AND THE BATTLE OF THE LABYRINTH
PERCY JACKSON AND THE LAST OLYMPIAN

THE DEMIGOD FILES
CAMP HALF-BLOOD CONFIDENTIAL

PERCY JACKSON AND THE GREEK GODS
PERCY JACKSON AND THE GREEK HEROES

HEROES OF OLYMPUS

PERCY JACKSON IS BACK!

Percy and his old friends from Camp Half-Blood join forces with new Roman demigods from Camp Jupiter for a deadly new mission: to prevent the all-powerful Earth Mother, Gaia, from awakening from her millennia-long sleep to bring about the end of the world.

THE LOST HERO
THE SON OF NEPTUNE
THE MARK OF ATHENA
THE HOUSE OF HADES
THE BLOOD OF OLYMPUS

THE DEMIGOD DIARIES

AN OLYMPIAN HAS FALLEN!

The god Apollo has been cast down from Olympus in the body of a teenage boy.
With the help of friends like Percy Jackson and familiar faces from
Camp Half-Blood, he must complete a series of harrowing trials to save
the world from a dangerous new enemy.

THE GODS OF EGYPT AWAKEN!

When an explosion shatters the ancient Rosetta Stone and unleashes Set, the
Egyptian god of chaos, only Carter and Sadie Kane can save the day. Their quest
takes the pair around the globe in a battle against the gods of Ancient Egypt.

THE GODS OF ASGARD ARISE!

After being killed in battle with a fire giant, Magnus Chase finds himself
resurrected in Valhalla as one of the chosen warriors of the Norse god Odin.
The gods of Asgard are preparing for Ragnarok – the Norse doomsday –
and Magnus has a leading role . . .

ABOUT THE AUTHOR

RICK RIORDAN, dubbed 'storyteller of the gods' by *Publishers Weekly*, is the author of five *New York Times* number-one bestselling book series with millions of copies sold throughout the world: Percy Jackson, the Heroes of Olympus and the Trials of Apollo, based on Greek and Roman mythology; the Kane Chronicles, based on Egyptian mythology; and Magnus Chase, based on Norse mythology. *Percy Jackson and the Lightning Thief*, Rick's first novel featuring the heroic young demigod, won the Red House Children's Book Award and is now a blockbuster film franchise starring Logan Lerman.

To learn more about Rick and his books, you can visit him at www.rickriordan.co.uk or follow him on Twitter @camphalfblood.